Arousal

ALSO BY MARTHA ROTH

Goodness

Mother Journeys:
Feminists Write about Mothering
Coedited with Maureen T. Reddy and Amy R. Sheldon

Transforming a Rape Culture
Coedited with Emilie Buchwald and Pamela R. Fletcher

Arousal

Bodies and Pleasures

MARTHA ROTH

MILKWEED
EDITIONS

© 1998, Text by Martha Roth

All rights reserved. Except for brief quotations in critical articles or reviews, no part of this book may be reproduced in any manner without prior written permission from the publisher: Milkweed Editions, 430 First Avenue North, Suite 400, Minneapolis, MN 55401

Distributed by Publishers Group West
Published 1998 by Milkweed Editions
Printed in the United States of America
Cover design by Tara Christopherson, Fruitful Results Design
Cover photo by Comstock Inc.
Interior design by Will Powers
The text of this book is set in Sabon.
98 99 00 01 02 5 4 3 2 1
First Edition

The epigraph on p. ix is from Michel Foucault, *History of Sexuality: An Introduction,* vol. 1 (New York: Random House, 1978), 157. Copyright © 1978 by Michel Foucault.

Milkweed Editions is a not-for-profit publisher. We gratefully acknowledge support from Elmer L. and Eleanor J. Andersen Foundation; James Ford Bell Foundation; Cray Research, a Silicon Graphics Company; Dayton's, Mervyn's, and Target Stores by the Dayton Hudson Foundation; Doherty, Rumble and Butler; Ecolab Foundation; General Mills Foundation; Honeywell Foundation; Jerome Foundation; McKnight Foundation; Andrew W. Mellon Foundation; Minnesota State Arts Board through an appropriation by the Minnesota State Legislature; Creation and Presentation Programs of the National Endowment for the Arts; Lawrence and Elizabeth Ann O'Shaughnessy Charitable Income Trust in honor of Lawrence M. O'Shaughnessy; Piper Jaffray Companies, Inc.; Ritz Foundation; John and Beverly Rollwagen Fund of the Minneapolis Foundation; St. Paul Companies, Inc.; Star Tribune/Cowles Media Foundation; James R. Thorpe Foundation; Lila Wallace-Reader's Digest Literary Publishers Marketing Development Program, funded through a grant to the Council of Literary Magazines and Presses; and generous individuals.

Library of Congress Cataloging-in-Publication Data
Roth, Martha.
    Arousal : bodies and pleasures / Martha Roth. — 1st ed.
        p. cm.
    Includes bibliographical references.
    ISBN 1-57131- 220-X (hardcover : alk. paper)
    I. Sexual excitement. 2. Sex (Psychology)   3. Cruelty.
  4. Violence.   I. Title.
BF692.R66   1998
155.3—dc21   97-45983
                                                              CIP

This book is printed on acid-free paper.

For Marty, inexhaustibly

Many people helped me to write this book, chief among them Emilie Buchwald, friend, colleague, and magnificent editor, and Carolee Schneemann, *chère amie* who has been thinking with me about these matters for many years. Ann B. Snitow told me casually that "sexual arousal is the most under-theorized topic in human psychology," and my friend and colleague Pamela R. Fletcher thought it would be a good subject for a book. Members of my writing group, past and present, have helped immeasurably: Maria Damon, Heid Erdrich, Pamela Fletcher, Helen Hoy, Carol A. Miller, Leslie Adrienne Miller, Valerie Miner, and Susan Welch. Friends who lent me their brains and hearts include Meena Alexander, Judith Arcana, Neda Miranda Blažević, Martha Boesing, Virgil Burnett, Patricia Cumbie, Lesley Ferris, the late Tom Jordan, Susan Kaplan, Tomoko Kuribayashi, Barbara Laslett, Deborah LeSueur, Jackie Marsh, Toni A. H. McNaron, John Mowitt, Diana O'Brien, Brian Rotman, Madelon Sprengnether, and Leslie Yoder. My children and husband remained cheerful and supportive throughout the difficult process of writing, as did my wonderful agent, Faith Hampton Childs.

Arousal

Introducing Arousal 3

Learning to Read 19

Sameness and Difference 29
    Mirrors and Frames
    Androgyny

Desire 45

Silence 63
    Screams
    Penis Envy

Cruelty 83
    Evil and Danger
    Pain and Blood
    Death

Fantasies of Fertility 109

Possibilities 125

Notes 145

Suggested Reading 153

We must not think that by saying yes to sex, one says no to power; on the contrary, one tracks along the course laid out by the general deployment of sexuality. It is the agency of sex that we must break away from, if we aim — through a tactical reversal of the various mechanisms of sexuality — to counter the grips of power with the claims of bodies, pleasures, and knowledges, in their multiplicity and their possibility of resistance. The rallying point for the counterattack against the deployment of sexuality ought not to be sex-desire, but bodies and pleasures.

        MICHEL FOUCAULT

Arousal

Introducing Arousal

WHEN A PEACOCK BECOMES AROUSED, the scraggly tail feathers that drag behind him in the dust gradually lift and separate. He trembles with effort as his dusty train parts and blooms, disclosing slender fringed coverts that support a minaret of feathers patterned with iridescent eyes. As the bird's tail jerks upward its movements grow smoother, the dust falls away, and the feathers sweep open in a pyramidal fan of green, gold, purple, and blue. Flaming up, the fan rises and rises until it dwarfs the peacock's body and becomes a display screen that he must balance carefully upon the delicate bones of his back, a breathtaking emblem of desire. Bronze-green and piercing blue, the eyes stare. Then, to summon the attention of anyone who might not be looking, the peacock shrieks.

Arousal

Arousal seems simple for peafowl: the male displays, the female chooses. So does the completion of the process: He covers her for a moment. Eggs are laid; chicks hatch.

There's nothing simple about human sexual arousal. In the first place, we now for the most part separate sexual pleasure from replenishing the species. In the second place, a river of language runs through each one of us, a fluid layer of symbol and concept intervening between us and our pleasures. Our strategies for attracting attention are full of contradictions: males display themselves and females smell aggression, competition, vanity. Females display ourselves and feel betrayed or cheapened into the strategic curve of breast on a glossy magazine cover. And if we do succeed in arousing a potential partner, then what?

Arousal is a fluid, unstable state, like the plasma phase of a gas. Scientists describe it in technical language: beginning phase, plateau phase. It inspires poets and artists to create miracles of praise. Lovers play with it, stretching the moment like a soap bubble. We delight in inventing pleasures and laugh at how beautiful we are: in the extraordinary physical well-being that accompanies arousal, we feel at the same moment kin to all creation and uniquely, pricelessly individual.

Human courtship has been studied, but sexual arousal, as far as it can be isolated, has not. We hold contradictory views: arousal is seen as a good, healthy thing and also a sinful remnant to be hidden or denied. While we may support freedom of speech and sexual expression, most of us discourage children and young people from arousing themselves or one another, and we surround adult arousal

Introducing Arousal

with strict regulations. We spend billions of dollars each year on books, magazines, pictures, perfumes, and toys that promise arousal, yet at the same time we imagine arousal as an enemy and try to protect ourselves against it with religious and civil laws.

We value sexual arousal as an expression of power and vitality, but in our contradictory way we also forbid, confine, and control the direction of our arousal response. For each of us a range of acceptable directions exists, and if we find ourselves responding "inappropriately"—lusting after children, for example, or exposing our bodies—we are punished by our own conscience and sometimes by laws. We love to compare our sexual urges to other animals', but we use our peculiar human powers to delay arousal and to distort or enhance it. Humans invented heterosexuality, homosexuality, celibacy, chastity, lyric poetry, sadism, and masochism.

We seem to believe that arousing lust is asking for trouble because other passions are always aroused as well. Our passions—the feelings that sweep over us and, in sweeping, change us—are like a nest of coiled serpents; when one awakens, they all stir. Women fear men's arousal as a prelude to assault. Men fear women's arousal as a hostile challenge to their manhood. Even those of us who are drawn to lovers of the same sex have tremendous anxiety about failures of arousal. Sexual arousal is a process that we fear and desire, joke about and hide, yet seldom question. Are we afraid of understanding our own arousal—afraid that if looked into it might show us secrets we would rather not know?

Arousal

One of my daughters once worked at a zoo, where the peacocks appeared to court her. Her office was in a trailer, and when she came out of her door a cock would shriek and trill and laboriously mount his splendid display, turning from side to side so she could admire him. She would smile and speak to him and go about her business. He would totter after her for as long as he could balance his offering on his twig-thin legs, then fold his fan and go back to scratching in the dust. Some days, she said, she felt a weird temptation. "No one else has ever shown me anything like that."

They have, of course; every human lover tries to display his best traits or hers. We may not have the feathers, but we can choose a wine or steal third.

But maybe a peacock's arousal is less simple than it looks. The energy that sometimes inspires a cock to spread his fan for courtship at other times leads him to unfurl and strut combatively in front of other males. Was my daughter being courted or challenged? Peacocks fight with their tails partly open, shrieking, scratching, and pecking as several birds join to attack one. Do they fight over hens? Do they fight out of boredom or fear?

Other creatures also make the same gestures in rut and in combat, including human beings. We show the same bodily changes when sexually aroused as when fighting or afraid: the heart pounds, the eyes shine, the skin prickles, we sweat and breathe faster. Penises and clitorises may throb and grow erect.

For these reasons, some serious thinkers conclude that in all animal species sexual arousal is tied to aggression.

Rape, in this view, is simply one extreme of sexual behavior, as "natural" as gentle courtship. People are animals, after all, and other male animals force themselves on females. Gangs of drakes chase ducks and knock them down; cats claw and snarl when they mate; wolves nip one another until they bleed; some insects even devour their mates.

People are animals, yes, but also something more, something self-conscious, guilty, and hungry for the divine. We are animals with languages and laws, books and churches and TV, and we use our sexuality for much more than keeping up our numbers. Freud's sexual theory named the source of human energy, our strength and our wounds, and "sexuality" now determines a large part of our social identity. We have taken the human desire for sexual pleasure and deployed it throughout our social life, as Michel Foucault writes in his *History of Sexuality*: "[S]ex gradually became an object of great suspicion; the . . . fragment of darkness that we each carry within us: a general signification, a universal secret, an omnipresent cause, a fear that never ends. . . ."

He called the process by which this happened, this gradual becoming, a "deployment" because once the notion of a sexual identity emerged, it was used against us. We became jerkoffs or nymphos, queers or lezzies, peepers or freaks, rather than people with certain bodies who seek certain pleasures. According to Foucault, we pinned our Enlightenment hopes for discovering the truth about human beings onto our sexual desires, believing that sexuality can be made to divulge the essential secrets of the person.

Arousal

After a painstaking historical analysis of how modern sexuality has been constructed, Foucault goes on to say,

> *One day, perhaps, in a different economy of bodies and pleasures, people will no longer quite understand how the ruses of sexuality, and the power that sustains its organization, were able to subject us to that austere monarchy of sex, so that we became dedicated to the endless task of forcing its secret, or exacting the truest of confessions from a shadow.*
>
> *The irony of this deployment is in having us believe that our "liberation" is in the balance.*

As I understand the last sentence, it refers to the claims of pornographers from the marquis de Sade to Larry Flynt that indulging extreme sexual desires can free an individual. Real human liberation, of course, would be a much more complex and far-reaching social process. Real liberation would mean our becoming conscious of the many ways in which we surrender power to institutions—to the medical or psychological establishment, for example, by accepting the sexual identities that have been forged for us—and freeing ourselves from "that austere monarchy of sex." We have now sexualized virtually every expenditure of human energy. We have invented "good" and "bad" sexualities, and we have devoted ourselves to finding the differences and jailing or rubbing out the "bad" part.

In the early 1990s, two colleagues and I collaborated on a book called *Transforming a Rape Culture*. We wanted to

Introducing Arousal

make a work of literature that would look at the crime of rape as an aberration in human behavior—a thwarted gesture, a grievous error—and one, as our title implies, that can be changed. We don't believe that men and women are doomed to sexual violence; we do believe that the connection between pleasure and cruelty is made, not born, in us, and that humans can move beyond rape—that rape, in other words, is not one extreme of human sexuality. The contributors to our book all shared their visions of how our species might begin to build a world without rape, changing our definitions of gender, family, schooling, law, and religion to break the tie between sexuality and violence, and a few of us tentatively confronted the vexed relationship of sensual pleasure to games of power, including fantasies of coercion, seduction, outright rape, and pain.

As part of our research for the book, we read masses of material describing sexual crimes. I was nauseated and saddened by the litany of assault and torture, the constant reminders that sexuality, particularly women's sexuality, is hated by both women and men. Yet I was also aroused, sexually kindled, by some of the violent material we read.

The words aroused me, not the actions. The few times when I've been threatened with sexual violence I've been terrified and furious. Nothing about the actual threat of cruelty made me want to repeat it, yet its image in words evoked pleasure. I recognized this contradiction: However much I wish it were otherwise, my vulnerable, pleasure-seeking self belongs to culture, and sexual arousal to violence and cruelty has been written into me.

Arousal

I want to believe that I can break this association and write a different story. Our corollary purpose in *Transforming a Rape Culture* was to hasten the day when people will welcome sexual pleasure without images of pain and coercion—when we will be distressed, not aroused, by tales of torture and bondage. Human beings have proved that we're not utter prisoners of our biology; we stand upright, create chemical elements, land on the moon. We have constructed our culture of eroticized violence out of many sources, over thousands of years, yet it does not seem too much to hope that we might begin to make a different one.

When I try to trace the link between pleasure and cruelty to its origin in my personal history, I come up against the banal fact that my erotic imagination was shaped by images from the Second World War. I was born in Chicago in 1938, the year the Germans invaded Czechoslovakia and the year before Sigmund Freud died. My mother worked in a Jewish social agency, and when she went back to work soon after I was born, she hired a young German-Jewish refugee as nursemaid. Lina looked after me until I could be sent to nursery school. My parents chose a progressive nursery school, run by Miss Bille and Miss Schuler, who were also refugees from Nazi-occupied Europe.

Safe in the American Midwest, we children played games set in the European theater of the war, at the ages of three and four shouting mouth-filling words like *bombardier, gestapo,* and *incendiary*. I remember playing

Introducing Arousal

"Air Raid" with twists of red and white crepe paper in the sandbox at Miss Bille's school. The white twists were ordinary bombs, and the red twists were *incendiary* bombs. We must have played some game of GIs and pinup girls; I have a hazy memory of throwing a tantrum one winter morning and refusing to wear snowpants because I wanted to show my legs. The sandbox was full of snow, and Miss Bille wouldn't let me play outside bare-legged with my friend Jon.

When I entered public kindergarten in 1943, some of my classmates came from refugee families. The summer when the war ended we were between first and second grade, but the games we played went on using it as a mise-en-scène. We didn't imagine the consequences of firebombing, any more than we knew what was at stake in our spy torture scenes or imagined genocide when we played cowboys and Indians. These were just the available settings for our games of dominance and submission: "Now I'll be the gestapo and you be the spy."

Among the thousands of people who had come to the United States as immigrants or refugees from Nazi-threatened Europe, of course, were many of the men and women associated with the young science of psychoanalysis. The tide of analysts flooded certain segments of American life, including the movies, and they brought a new vocabulary and a new discourse of infantile sex and violence. Obsession, compulsion, and the Oedipus complex became household words in some homes, like ours.

I don't know whether my nursemaid Lina ever stroked my genitals to quiet me, but my earliest memory,

Arousal

from before nursery school, was of the solacing pleasure of an orgasm. Something about the way images of the war reached me placed it as erotic, and I did absorb the message that genital pleasure should be secret. The tie of pleasure to secrecy fed into the concept of espionage, and fantasies of attracting Jon with my bare legs gave way to fantasies of myself as a captured spy or Jew or Jewish spy, being interrogated by tall Germans in leather coats.

Other writers, like Erica Jong and Alix Kates Shulman, have described the nazification of their erotic imaginations, but I suspect the specific details don't matter. Whatever may be going on in the world during the years when a human child acquires culture, the coiled serpents of lust and rage sleep in our cultural reservoir of images, the *imaginary* that Roland Barthes called "the unconsciousness of the unconscious," which underlies thought and language. Before a young child knows to name her or his desire for genital pleasure, it has already taken shape, and the shapes of arousal and pleasure are already twinned with rage. Many people have no conscious awareness of this shaping. In them, the rage sleeps deeply. But it is always there.

By itself this twinning won't explain sexual violence. We have all been stamped by culture, but we're not all rapists or child molesters. It isn't useful to ask whether such violence is "instinctual" or "learned": Human beings always act out of some calculus of our genetic inheritance and our conditions of life.

No human behavior has a single cause. We begin to become distinctively human before we're born, and all our experiences help to form our personalities along the axis of our genetic potential. Our behavior is constructed by these influences, and most of it is multidetermined, over-determined, by overlapping, reinforcing lessons carried in the foods our mothers ate and the music they listened to, the drugs they took and the settings where they bore us, religion, law, nutrition, schooling, medicine, TV, background radiation, our peers, our work, our play, and our luck.

Human intelligence being the fabulously inventive trait that it is, I believe we're not prisoners of our image reservoir and that it's possible to intervene, substitute, unravel, and rebuild our own responses and even our language. We can influence the contents of our imaginary, not by criminal sanctions or religious precepts or *Clockwork Orange*-style behavioral conditioning, but by remaking culture within us. In *Pornography and Silence,* Susan Griffin suggests that we can begin to loosen the tie between pleasure and rage by understanding and acknowledging the flesh of the helpless child we were when we first knew pleasure. I will try to reach that understanding through language—the smooth, corrupted words of English in which I read, write, speak, hear, think, and become aroused.

My violent fantasies went underground as I matured, and when sex became real, its playful fantasy elements changed. In college I acquired some political sophistication along with what passed in those days for a sexual initiation among American adolescents. My new fantasy persona was that of a bohemian free spirit, a woman who took

Arousal

lovers lightly and easily; she was serious about free love and equal rights and never indulged in games where she might have to play the role of a victim. I became a democratic socialist in the 1950s, read Mary Wollstonecraft, J. S. Mill, and Frederick Engels, and talked about the Woman Question.

This new role was my attempt to straighten out some of the emotional complexities of sex and love. I didn't know how they were related, except that when I "fell in love" with someone, I wanted sexual pleasure with that person. I didn't understand gender or power in relation to pleasure. I thought that all I had to do to slip the leash of culture was to assert sexual independence, and that my partners could do the same. If we were careful to avoid the dangers of pregnancy and disease, we thought, like generations before us, that we could be free. We aroused each other easily, with no sense that our play had been scripted for us. We thought we could remake the world without first remaking it in ourselves.

For as long as I can remember, since I was a small child, my body has gone through cycles of arousal on its own, helplessly. Once, its demands clamored: walking would become difficult and I would have to masturbate— in the toilet, in the kitchen against the edge of a chairback, sitting on a commuter train; sometimes in dangerous places—a museum, a movie theater, a schoolroom, a friend's living room, any place where I could be alone for a few minutes. Did the risk of discovery heighten my arousal?

With time, arousal's claims have muted. I try to stay open to cues—images, music, words, scents, or colors—that trigger the process as I dig and weed in the garden, go to library or market, cook, carry laundry up and down stairs, wash dishes, ride on airplanes. Descriptions of violent sex sometimes arouse me, even a headline glimpsed in a newspaper, but other things, too: the smell of peppermint or pine released by the hot sun, or a whiff of scent, silky dark hair on some stranger's forearm, uncovered when he rolls up a shirtsleeve, a scrap of Scarlatti or Jelly Roll Morton. Then I touch myself, and a familiar cascade of feeling flows from my fingers. It disturbs me that my closest approach to ecstasy should include desires that figure what is otherwise called hell.

It isn't just me, of course. Humans have used all our resources of language and art in an attempt to be worthy of the iridescent sweep of arousal, but at the same time some of us feel degraded, brought to earth, especially if we have taken on the burden of biblical stories about serpents, gardens, women, and men.

Long before the Bible, in prehistoric times, small clusters of people worshiped a great goddess. Following the work of Marija Gimbutas, most scholars now agree that early human societies worshiped female fertility, probably in the form of an earth goddess. The traces of goddess worship were swept away by "nomadic pastoralists from the North," as Riane Eisler calls the believers in a single male sky god. From stone images found in many different excavation sites, scholars have guessed that vulva and

Arousal

phallus were sacred to the goddess, and that perhaps the exquisite sensations found in them were believed to be her gifts.

The sensitive erectile organs of our pleasure have long disappeared from Western sacred imagery. In Hindu observance, lingam (phallus) and yoni (vulva) are holy images, and genitals figure prominently in sacred representations of other cultures from Asia, Africa, and Oceania. On a few ancient Irish churches the sheela-na-gig can still be seen, a female gargoyle stretching wide the lips of her vulva. The squat, eyeless stone figurines found in European and Middle Eastern excavations, of which the Willendorf Venus is the best known, are generally believed to be idols of the goddess worshipers. Some of them are decorated with images of the vulva. When were genital images purged? They're now seen either as rude jokes or as dwelling-places for demonic violence and destruction. When folk worshiped the goddess, perhaps sexuality was sacred; perhaps arousal was a form of prayer.

This reflection on bodies and pleasures is an attempt to resolve some of my own contradictory feelings about sexual arousal as well as a vision of how human beings might begin to remake ourselves sexually, restocking the cultural imaginary so that what we call sexuality is a welcome part of life, neither a bothersome evolutionary remnant nor a huge totem before which we lie prostrate. The sexual impulse is usually described as a powerful disordering force, and we marshal a lot of our psychic energy to direct and control it. What if we could remake a psychic equilibrium that would, as Foucault says, "counter the grips of power with the claims of bodies, pleasures, and knowledges, in their multiplicity and their possibility of resistance"? What if we could use this deep old pleasure to discover new kinds of order and stability instead of spending energy on restraining our sexuality?

In this book I'll test my vision of a liberated future by reading the history of my own body—my training in arousal and pleasure through language, images, and relationships—against the history of my consciousness of that tangle of desire and conflict that we call sexuality. To support my belief in a transformed future against a global information industry that continually deploys sexuality, spewing out stories and pictures of sexualized violence and violent sexuality, I have only my knowledge that humans made this culture. We can—if we choose—begin to make a different one.

Learning to Read

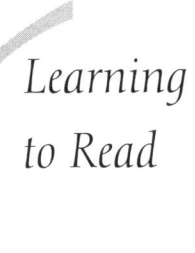

Behind a thicket of black print
Something stirs
Some beast, its red heart's blood
Squeezed into words

A beast is born and dies on every page
Its blood gone black
The printed letters are its cage
And not its track

I DON'T REMEMBER ANYTHING that happened before I could speak, but when I was about thirty-five and wrote this verse I could still recall, dimly and in spurts, what the world looked like before

Arousal

I could read. Writing seemed to be the key to understanding everything. Letters were a secret grown-ups knew, a vast cipher, and I was mad to crack the code.

So much is hidden from children, so many mysteries must be solved. Psychoanalytic philosophers say that the Big Mystery of childhood goes back to our parents' sexual organs, glamorous, privileged, concealed, and that sexual curiosity and the sense of awe probably stem from the same wonder. If this is true, then I displaced this curiosity onto written language.

Small children know the pleasure of touching their own smooth genitals but can hardly imagine how their bodies or their pleasures will transform in adulthood. At the core of many religions are transformative mysteries: the Eleusinian rites; the mystical Trinity; the spirits that dwell in sacred substances, in bread, in wine; the wrapped Torah inside the ark, the text inside the mezuzah. Many mystical practices involve manipulation of sacred words.

Sacred texts of the three major monotheisms, Judaism, Christianity, and Islam, are written in priestly languages. Merlin Stone, in *When God Was a Woman,* says the great goddesses Ninlil, Dir, and Ishtar were also goddesses of writing. For centuries, literacy was a privilege reserved for priests. In our time, we all get a chance to solve one of the great mysteries.

Language, of course, is itself a code, and words stimulate and comfort us long before we learn to read. The spoken word can be powerfully arousing; lovers give great phone. But reading one can do alone. Long before I even dreamed of sex with other people, I could read.

Reading is unnatural, addictive self-pleasuring, but a high cultural value attaches to it, while nowadays chaste illiteracy is a source of shame. Reading is a secret that we're encouraged to find out, a permitted transgression. Mastering the signs of written language gave me access to myself, aroused my senses. I felt that I read with my whole face, all my sense organs, and my eyes had an erotic relation to the page. In *The Pleasure of the Text,* his book about the erotics of reading, Roland Barthes says that because we respond to it physically, all reading/writing "approaches" pornography. I trained for arousal by learning to read. Barthes writes, "The text is a fetish object, and *this fetish desires me."* It certainly places itself in my hands.

When my father put me to bed, he told me stories from the *Iliad,* quite violent ones, about the priest Laocoön and his sons who were attacked by a sea serpent, and about the men inside the wooden horse who crept out at night and slaughtered their trusting Trojan hosts. When my mother tucked me in, she read to me until she suspected that I could do it for myself. I protested, but she was firm.

A favorite book eased the weaning: *Greek Myths,* a telling of Bullfinch's *Tales from the Greek Anthology.* I fought the loss of my mother's sofa, the warmth of her body, the stories unrolling in her low voice; I stumbled over long words and proper names. But *Greek Myths* had simple words and line drawings that I found beautiful, of curvy girls and angular boys all dressed in pleated chitons and with statuesque blank eyes. I loved the stories of sex and violence—especially Proserpina, wildflowers spilling from her hands as she was caught around the waist by the

Arousal

god of the underworld, and Narcissus, who fell in love with his reflection in a clear, still pool. Leaning forward to kiss the beautiful reflected mouth, he fell into the pool and drowned.

I could find some words—the ones I knew by heart—in the printing on the page and so fell into the pool myself, drowning (as it seems to me now) in the fluid of text and story. If the pool had been a mirror, or a page, Narcissus might have entered it and met his other self. The page yielded to my eye, opening into wonders that quickened my blood while leaving me safe in my chair. Its surface seemed to me a permeable zone, something like the invisible membrane that separated this world from Hades. Pluto and Proserpina—and I—traveled back and forth; why not Narcissus?

Barthes might have been looking at the illustration of Proserpina when he wrote, "[W]hat pleasure wants is the site of a loss, the seam, the cut, the deflation, the *dissolve* which seizes the subject in the midst of bliss. Culture thus recurs as an edge: in no matter what form." The culture he writes about is one in which Proserpina's rape is viewed as pleasure. While a girl-child gains power by learning the complicated tasks of reading for pleasure, she also learns culture and its edges, its false mirrorings, its assumption that sauce for the gander—abduction and forced sex—tastes good to the goose. Before I knew it, the erotic tentacles of these tales and Grimm's and Andersen's and Perrault's, tales of seduction, rape, torture, and murder, wound me securely onto the skein of culture so that I never questioned how a man can fall in love with a sleeping woman nor why Bluebeard murdered his wives.

These tales of violent transformation belonged to childhood, to the intense and private early work of wresting satisfaction from books. By the time reading became social again, something to achieve in school or share with friends, I put them away. My friends and I read everything we could get our hands on, and though at first most children's stories were insipid compared to the strong stuff of myth and fairy tale, we soon found reflections of our own lives and desires in robust, old-fashioned books like *Little Women* and *Rebecca of Sunnybrook Farm.* Their young girl heroes had adventures and punishments, and no babyish magic rescued them. They got angry; they felt abandoned; they solved problems in a world of parents, sisters, uncles, and aunts—distant enough for comfort, but recognizable.

We loved books about dogs and horses, especially when the noble creatures were threatened with vivisection or the glue factory. Comic books packed even more punch, but their stories were always the same. Then we discovered the deployment of sex on the covers of paperback novels, years before *Lady Chatterley's Lover* or *Tropic of Cancer* could be sold in the United States. We had to make do with a paltry supply of racy pocketbooks, most of them coming from a rack in a corner store owned by an irascible old couple named Klein.

I remember them as old; they were probably in their forties in the 1940s. Minnie Klein died before neighborhood redevelopment claimed their store and I grew up and

Arousal

moved away. Still, in dreams and memories that street corner and that dim, cluttered store seem very close, just around some corner of the air. If I really tried, I could get back to it, on the ground floor of the white-tile brick building where the McNultys and the Hickses lived, with its window displays of shabby toys and comic books, protected from the sun in summer by a sheet of amber plastic.

Sid Klein's shrill "Get outta here!" sounded throughout my childhood, although he must have done most of his business with my friends and me. We were in his store every day, buying comics, penny candies, vanilla or cherry Cokes, little wax bottles of colored syrups. (You bit the top off the bottle and sucked out the syrup; then, if you could stand it, you chewed the wax.) In the back, where we seldom had an excuse to go, Klein's sold condoms, and vaginal creams to use with diaphragms, soberly displayed behind glass. We would sneak to the back of the store and point and giggle, and Sid would scream, "Get outta here or I'll tell your parents!"

The paperbacks had bright covers. Names of the "good" books circulated among us like samizdat: *The Amboy Dukes, Studs Lonigan, Meg, The Foxes of Harrow.* How many of us were pulled into reading literature by our interest in arousal? Some of us just read the "good" parts, the scenes of wonder, discovery, and (chaste by post-*Lady Chatterley* standards) lovemaking. Some of us were snared by the author's voice.

Print enters my brain as subtly as a gas, transforming my imagination and my body without any barrier, no decision needed. Our house was full of books, and my parents encouraged me to sample them. I remember staying up late when I babysat with my brother, smoking stolen cigarettes and reading H. G. Wells's *Island of Dr. Moreau* or Aldous Huxley's *Brave New World*. Science fiction, mysteries (there were always three or four from the rental library, their jackets covered in clear plastic), and horror stories held more promise of secret knowledge and chilled my flesh on hot summer nights. I became one of those hopeless print addicts who reads books and magazines, newspapers and pamphlets, labels and cereal boxes, and the fine print on package inserts.

In my teens I discovered poetry, some of it frankly erotic, though almost all of it written by men. When I started playing at pleasure with young men, I tried to write erotica from a female perspective, to counter the fact that all of the sexually explicit books and poems I had read reflected sexual pleasure in terms of male bodies and dynamics. I made a few tries in stories and poems, but the task was beyond me. I thought I might be a writer when I grew up.

In the sixties my nonviolent feminist friends and I used to talk about a "liberated pornography." Why couldn't there be an erotic literature in which power relations are not sexualized and sexuality isn't deployed; in which bodies and pleasures are all that matter? Men don't have to be rapists or fantasists of pain; women don't have to be virgins, victims, or dominatrixes. We tried to imagine sexy stories in which all the characters have fun.

Arousal

There's a lot of lesbian and gay erotica now, for which some writers deliberately choose politically liberatory stories, and some of it is pretty stimulating. But I'm still waiting for hot heterosexual feminist erotica. Catharine MacKinnon has argued—although I hope she is wrong—that male/female sex so deeply encodes dominance/submission that we cannot imagine our way out of these relations. Heterosexual feminist painters and photographers have done better than writers so far, maybe because they can concentrate on imagery without the burden of narrative words.

Feminist visions for perfecting the world usually include a sexual revolution in which women and men can be equal partners, and pleasure is completely untied from childbearing. Political revolutions have always betrayed this vision because "gender justice" has never been the primary goal. However idealistic the commitment of young revolutionaries to reordering the social priorities that keep women down, the pull of old narratives, old satisfactions, has been too strong. Lynne Segal says about the failure of sixties movements, "The defeat of attempts to build a caring and equal society dragged down with it feminist hopes for women's sexual liberation."

Our discussions of liberated erotica always ran aground, because we always came up against a sense of the hatred packed into lust, the rage that demands fantasies of tyranny, treachery, and blood. After all, we were still swimming in the second wave of feminism. Perhaps now, after twenty years or more of increasingly sophisticated thinking about gender and language, our imaginations might range freely and deeply enough to reach back for the primitive mysteries and pleasures of reading, to its carnal connection.

Sameness and Difference

Mirrors and Frames

NARCISSUS WAS A MAN DYING for the love of beauty, or its likeness. As I puzzled my way into language and representation, myths and mirrors, I was drawn to the suggestions of trickery, doubleness, and danger in the notion of mirroring. I knew a pair of twins who looked enough alike to enjoy confusing their friends. The word *likeness* meant not the thing itself but a close replica, close enough to fool others. I read a horror story about someone who met himself in the street. Perseus was able to kill the dread Medusa when he could aim at her in reflection. The pool lured Narcissus to his death.

Psychoanalyst Jacques Lacan teaches that human consciousness begins in the moment when we first see ourselves seen by another, reflected in another's gaze—usually

Arousal

our mother's. The mirror shows us a further split, *I* and *me,* seeing and seen. We split into watcher and watched, subject and object. First our consciousness is born, then our self-consciousness, and we become more wary after each split.

I spent long secret minutes in front of the bathroom mirror, wrapping myself glamorously in bath towels and improvising dramatic monologues. Where did my notions of glamour come from, at five and six and seven? Mainly from *Life* magazine pictures of GI pinups or USO canteens—the show-biz images of World War II that alternated with grim white-eyed shots of battle and, after 1944, with images of Nazi atrocities.

The war provided those twin anchors for erotic feelings: the provocative display of women's bodies and images of violent death. As a female child, I had been taught since infancy to be concerned with how I looked; as a Jew, I was or very recently had been a potential victim of violence. I knew I had to keep erotic pleasure secret. In the towel scenes, I was often a beautiful spy on a secret mission or arguing my way out of certain death.

Sometimes I imagined traveling across the mirror's surface into another side of the space in which I lived. In *Through the Looking Glass* Alice says, "It's the same as far as you can see; beyond that, everything's different." Her adventure is a nice metaphor for what happens when you lose yourself in the private pleasure of reading, both scary and delicious. If I could glide through that literal reflecting surface perhaps another part of my life, perhaps another me, would be revealed.

Sameness and Difference

The mirror also offered a refuge, a playground where ordinary rules didn't keep. I gazed at an image of my own face blooming in a familiar place, but unfamiliar, too—shadowed, tinted, reversed, tantalizing. Fertile ground for fantasy, the mirror taught me to gaze into frames. The origin of painting, of image making, says critic Jacques Derrida, is in the Narcissus myth. The artist falls in love with his/her own reflection. Like most children, I spent hours drawing pictures—of people, mainly women, with elaborate hair and dress. They weren't me; they were women I wanted to see and didn't—big strong figures, women of power and beauty.

On Sundays my father took me to museums—the Museum of Science and Industry, the Field Museum of Natural History, and the Art Institute, where I learned that the subjects of art are violence and sex, fear and desire. I didn't say this to my father, and he didn't say it to me, but I saw the tortured bodies of gods and saints and the achingly cuppable breasts of marble statues.

I had to invent the heroines of my drawings. Big, strong beautiful women are still hard to find. There was Wonder Woman, of course, but she was firmly framed in the small cheap pages of comic books. The women of ballet and theater fascinated me, their boxed images on a proscenium stage seen usually from the second balcony as a birthday or Christmas treat. Perhaps the Narcissus story is the origin of performance, too.

My mother's uncle was a producer in the Yiddish theater and an officer of the Theatrical Managers, Agents, and Treasurers, a union that included box-office employees.

Arousal

When Uncle Ed came to Chicago to tour a Yiddish production and visit his sister, my grandmother, he sprinkled theater tickets around the family for whatever happened to be playing. My parents had a high regard for the "legitimate" theater and for the famous actresses who brought their New York hits to Chicago—Katharine Cornell, Lynn Fontanne, Judith Anderson, Uta Hagen—and they often took me along. From somewhere (maybe Uncle Ed) I learned that actresses had unconventional sex lives; they had lovers and often didn't marry. I didn't learn until much later that some were lesbians.

Theater held an erotic charge. The bright square of the stage, the real people moving and speaking, and the flecks swimming in beams of colored light were fraught with glamour so sharp as to be almost painful. I saw *Carmen Jones* and *Oklahoma!* and loved the sounds of a live orchestra and the amazing freedom of dancers' bodies.

Movies lacked the glamour of theater; they were ordinary and intimate as dreams. Part of theater's thrill was its split reality, its open secret. You always knew you were sitting at a play, while movies shamelessly engulfed you. My mother thought they were low class. You had to be beautiful and talented to command a theaterful of people from a stage. My father told me that movie acting wasn't really acting, that it was all in the camera. It seemed to me that movies didn't play fair—they seized your eyes and you had no choice.

An entire field of feminist film criticism is now built on the notion of the gaze, the camera-controlled process by which you, the viewer, objectify the heroine and recognize her as not-you, the Other. For women, according to critic Laura Mulvey, watching movies always means a split in consciousness as we identify with both male subject and object. It does for men, too—at least for most men, in most movies. Like dreams, movies shift us around. Gazing at the screen, perhaps we revisit the moment Lacan described; perhaps we keep coming back to the movies hoping that someday we will melt into the image, healing our cloven selves.

The gaze is essentially male, according to Mulvey and the critics who follow her analysis, although both men and women can possess it, and, in theory at least, both can be gazed at. In practice, except for action movies and gay male films, both men and women mostly gaze at women. A gay director like Gus Van Sant makes us acutely aware of this gaze in his films *My Own Private Idaho* and *To Die For*, where the object of the gaze is a lovely young man. In *To Die For*, although Nicole Kidman plays a beautiful and seductive woman, the traditional object of the gaze, Van Sant is more interested in the young male actor Joaquin Phoenix, and directs our gaze with his camera. Is the actor "feminized" because his fuzzy body hair, his throat, his chest and arms and back are so caressed by the camera, so offered for the spectator?

Women also participate in the gaze that reduces female bodies to objects. Does the shared public fantasy of film make us all into androgynes, able to pass at will between observation and identification, between the bodies and actions of desirable men as well as women? Or is there a special pleasure for all women in gazing at a woman's body?

Arousal

Maybe women allow ourselves to enjoy gazing at the naked bodies of other women because in our culture of compulsory heterosexuality, desire itself is construed as masculine. For a woman to become aroused by another woman's body is seen as no more remarkable than the psychic contortions of the masquerade she performs when fitting herself into the niche of the Object of Desire.

Freud wrote that while men desire women, women desire men's desire for them. A woman thus becomes the *sign* of desire, rather than a person with desires. A note in the book *This Sex Which Is Not One,* by feminist psychoanalyst Luce Irigaray, calls this "an alienated or false version of femininity" that stands between a woman and her frank acknowledgment of desire. A conventionally feminine woman, according to Irigaray, wears "the masquerade" that makes her "experience desire not in her own right but as the man's desire situates her."

As a child I was aware of the masquerade, if not the sexual drama of power and desire. Certainly in film and in theater there was always a gap between the way women and girls were represented and what I saw in my mother and her friends and knew about myself. The women I knew were smart and strong and also good; they made jokes and decisions as well as dessert. I didn't exactly have the force of character at eight or nine to do much about the gap, but I decided to become an actress so that I could make my own images of women on the stage.

I was fifteen before I ever acted in a play, and by then my stakes in performance changed: like most teenage girls I wanted to be looked at and admired, and I didn't fully understand that wanting to be admired had typecast me. Simply being on a stage was physically arousing, but I still had a reforming zeal about performing: I wanted to play real women. Method acting was in vogue in the fifties, and my heroes were Kim Stanley, Barbara Bel Geddes, Rita Gam—actresses who tried to escape the masquerade, or parts of it at least, and bring a fuller sense of women's lives to the stage.

But after a few years of acting in college plays and little theaters, I realized again how limiting were the roles men wrote for women. Actresses still deplore the lack of meaty roles, even though some of them now have the power to commission scripts and get plays produced or movies made. I'm remembering life before Ellen Burstyn, Barbra Streisand, or Jodie Foster.

Once I played a Dublin hooker in a one-act play by Sean O'Casey. When I got into trouble, the director said carelessly, "Oh, you know, just do it like a hooker would."

I was a middle-class girl of sixteen and committed to answering the Woman Question. How the hell did I know how a hooker would act? Yet theater—and not just this particularly thick student director—assumed that all women replicated all other women's behavior; that our motives and actions were limited to those few subjects male playwrights chose to write about, mainly either snaring or rejecting men's sexual attention. In George Eliot's words, "Every woman is supposed to have the same set of motives, or else to be a monster." God knew I was interested in male attention, but I was a rotten actress because

Arousal

I couldn't imagine the gestures of a woman for whom it was not just an interest but a livelihood.

Most of the trouble came from the conflict at the heart of my desire to act. A performing woman is on display, selling herself, and this excited me, but I also wanted to expand the possibilities for women's performance. I wanted to act, I just didn't want to act like a "woman."

Ten years passed. I was married, still living in Chicago, and directing a play at a little theater, a Jacobean revenge tragedy. One night the phone rang. I shifted the baby to my left hip and picked up the receiver. "'Tis a pity you're a fuckin' whore," said a voice, a man's voice, tenor, with an Appalachian flavor.

I slammed down the phone. This was the winter of 1964; my husband was a graduate student. We had a small daughter and I was pregnant. At the next rehearsal for my production of John Ford's *'Tis Pity She's a Whore*, I told the three women in the cast about my phone call, and all three told me they'd had similar calls. The neighborhood section of a city paper had carried a publicity photo, identifying us by name. He—the Redneck—called me again, three or four times. All four of us women received obscene misspelled notes in the mail.

We were big girls, big-city girls; we shrugged off the episode. These things happen. There are a lot of crazy people in the world, some of them religious fundamentalists (although this was decades before the Religious Right emerged in its present form), and public speech was more prudish than it is now. The newspaper that ran our photo wouldn't even publish the full name of the play, and we traded stories about a New York production that had met the same fate, listed as *'Tis Pity She's a. . . .* The play dated from the early seventeenth century, its language was difficult, and its themes of incest and intrigue barely emerged from the overgrowth of Ford's heated lyricism. We sold out all our performances.

Our unknown harassers and the success of the show were connected, of course, by the magic of that charged word, *whore*. When a stranger's voice spoke the word into my ear, my very first response—before revulsion, before anger—was guilt: I've been found out. Any woman in the theater was open to the charge because she put her body on display. People, men, paid to look at her. She aroused their passions. The guilty secret was what drew me to theater in the first place.

Androgyny

In the fifties, when I was an undergraduate at the University of Chicago, I had a boyfriend who liked to explore odd, raffish corners of the city. He introduced me to a group of old people who hung out in a coffee shop on the Near North Side; they were the remnants of the Dill Pickle Club, originally friends of the poet and novelist Maxwell Bodenheim, a notorious bohemian and radical of the twenties. All of the survivors were poor and some in ill health. In the twenties and thirties they had been flaming iconoclasts. Now they were three or four old women with swollen ankles and untidy gray hair and two or three old

Arousal

men with bleared eyes and run-over shoes. They met on Saturday nights in the cheap, fluorescent-lit coffee shop as they had met before in speakeasies and studios; the decor may have been Edward Hopper, but the spirit was Emma Goldman.

Once upon a time, these people breathed the fires of free love and atheism and smashed the icons of good taste and polite behavior. Now they coughed and wheezed, keeping up with each others' diseases. "Hear about Dorothy? She had a stroke." "Ed's not doing too well, either." Drinkers of bootleg hooch, smokers of hashish, believers in internationalism and vers libre, they had written manifestoes and flaunted their pro-queer, antiracist sympathies. Max Bodenheim was dead in a New York slum, but they survived to meet once a week in the coffee shop where they drank Sanka and cadged Lucky Strikes from my boyfriend.

As the evening progressed, their bent shoulders would relax, their necks would straighten and their heads come up, a little color glowing in their cheeks and lips. As if it fell from the ceiling, they would pull around themselves some shreds of the glamour of their youth. They enchanted my boyfriend, but they left me cold; I couldn't appreciate their faded, heroic flagrancies.

One of the disturbing things about these people was that whatever their sexuality had been—lesbian, gay, bi, or straight—as they aged they were losing their gender markers, the strong differentiation of male and female in which I, at seventeen, at last felt secure. These ancients were wrinkled and flabby, with roughened voices and inconvenient hair—too little on their heads, too much sprouting from nostrils or ears or veiling the women's cheeks. They faced me with a truth about human aging long before I was ready to understand it: As we survive past childbearing, and our bodies stop brewing sex hormones as fiercely as they did in youth, we become less different, more merely human, as when we first slid into the world, smooth and slick.

In that same coffee shop, late on another night, I met my first drag queen, a slender young white man who oozed sensuality helplessly, regardlessly. His manner was cool as he told us about his recent masquerades. "And then this one truck driver slung his arm around my neck and said, 'Hey, honey, how'd you like to come home with me?'"

I could scarcely keep my hands away from him. I yearned for him, coveted him; I felt an ache in my breastbone that choked my voice, my laughter. I wanted him and I wanted to *be* him; I wanted to roll my girl's body out into the sliver of his. I felt the movements of his neat hands, his arched eyebrows, his mouth, as though they were my own, and every word he spoke, every move he made, aroused me. He put his hand on my boyfriend's wrist and whispered something in his ear, an ear that I knew with my own tongue. I was fascinated by the notion that he and I were competing for Danny. He could have Danny; I wanted *him*.

What did I want him for? A pet, I think; a costume, a body to slip into; what I felt was close to worship, close to obsession. I knew his nipples lay flat on his chest, like medallions set in marble. I knew the fine join of his knees.

Arousal

I could see myself stalking him, hounding him until I got what I wanted.

But I never figured out what that might be. I never met him again; but Danny and I talked about him, and he made a fantasy third in our group of two. He turned us both on, aroused our senses. Now I think I craved his brazen sexuality. By being a man who performed a woman, he embodied opportunities that felt closed to me, with my unambiguous breasts and hips. The old people's sexual identities had seemed rubbed, faint, indeterminate; his was multiple and sharp.

A later boyfriend, another scene: one of his close friends is a butch woman named Sherry who courts me, boasting, flirting, showing me how strong she is. I laugh and flirt back. "She's okay," Sherry tells my boyfriend, but I have the sense that she is doing more than vetting me, and I find myself aroused—although I don't want Sherry. Another night: a gay male friend and I pick up a boy we both dig, but we're too drunk to get it on. Another night: my lover and I go to a jazz club with a couple of friends, a lesbian and a gay man. The music arouses us and we decide to go to bed together, all four. We dissolve in laughter when the gay friend says, "Now tell me, what exactly are we going to *do?*"

I'm trying to grasp a dream of someone who stands outside gender—a being who is sensual but not reproductive, a being who eludes the different scripts of power and routine that threaten to delimit the lives of gendered people. A being like Shakespeare's Ariel, only with a sex life.

Novelist and transgender activist Leslie Feinberg says,

"Two genders aren't enough to define us all—and it's *not our fault.*" When we're young and at the mercy of strong impulses, we suffer from the straitness of those definitions, but one of the gifts of age is that they loosen with time and tinkering. The ambiguities that bugged me with the old Dill Pickle crowd can be, I see now, a comfort.

Plato, in the *Symposium*, a long, hard-drinking conversation about love, has the playwright Aristophanes tell the myth of the androgynes. Once upon a time, says Aristophanes, human beings were double creatures, with two heads and two bodies. Some were double men, some double women, and some combined a man and a woman. We were happy, so happy that the gods envied us, and Zeus punished us with a cataclysm by splitting us in two. Now we're incomplete, partial, lacking half our selves, and we can't rest until we find the one that was wrenched away from us, which is why some of us try out so many partners. ("No one believes this myth," says Wayne Koestenbaum in *The Queen's Throat*. "But it explains opera, which no one believes either.")

When we fall in love, we imagine that we've solved the puzzle, found a combination of sameness and difference that completes our missing parts, supplies the half that was torn away to leave us aching with desire. For a space of time, desire is stilled; we have everything we want. Freud called lovers "a group of two," but to the lovers themselves it feels more like restoration of that original doubleness that Aristophanes described, being two-in-one. Whatever their basis of attraction, a couple feels sufficient, slaked.

While I was writing this chapter and dreaming about

Arousal

androgyny, I came across a depressing piece of news: The Danish toy company that makes Legos announced that after forty successful years, it has changed the product. Sales have leveled off, or perhaps even decreased, and market research has determined that what's needed is a line of "girls' Legos" in pastel colors, with curving parts and tiny figures that have more expressive faces and bodies than the old abstract Lego people.

"What's happened is that girls have gone back to being girls," a sales manager was quoted as saying, as though border-crossing worldwide advertising, whose purpose is to make people want new things, had nothing to do with his job. The sales manager went on to say that in the 1940s, when Legos were first made and sold in Scandinavia, children's clothes and toys were androgynous, not aimed at and labeled for the use of one gender exclusively. Now that fad has passed, and parents and children want toys with strong marks of gender difference.

My heart sank when I read this item on the business page. It seems to me that most small children enjoy playing with a wide range of toys—stuffed animals, dolls, trucks, musical instruments, blocks, pencils and crayons, masks and dress-up clothes, trains, tools, makeup kits, finger paints, kitchen utensils, clay, water, and sand. Then between the ages of five and ten, in our culture they enter a phase in which they want to be segregated by gender, the years of "boys against girls" polarity. This desire to be with same-sex playfellows is heavily influenced by homophobic anxiety from adults around them and from the culture at large.

Sameness and Difference

These are the years when parents worry whether their children are acquiring the right social markers—for boys, sports; for girls, concern with their appearance ("the masquerade"). A four-year-old boy can dress up in long skirts and funny hats; no one will worry if he seems to prefer drawing and painting to playing catch, or if he likes to dance; but a nine-year-old boy who does these things risks being labeled as odd, "different," "girlie," "queer." Culture pits the "sexes" against one another, defining masculinity in terms of not-femininity, and charging the words *girl* and *woman* with emasculating disdain. The Lego company, of course, has a vested interest in shoring up these misogynistic, homophobic distinctions, because it can sell more Legos if boys must have boys' sets and girls, girls' sets. Just how many brave parents are going to buy for their young sons a set of toys packaged in pink and aqua and labeled "Lego Girls"?

Although in schools and play groups some lip service is usually paid to equality, this separation means inequality: boys must be separated from girls so they can grow into men. Men need to distinguish themselves clearly from women because—because—well, dammit, they just do. Of course, this arrangement robs both boys and girls. Why can't boys enjoy the same wide range of play as girls? Why can't boys play with new kinds of Legos—pink, lavender, aqua, pale green, round, crescent-shaped, ringlike, sinuous?

In fundamentalist reasoning, men's gender identities must be rigidly defined and separated from women's. Nature and the Bible are invoked to justify the separation.

Arousal

Anything that blurs it, even a lavender toy, threatens the whole structure of privilege and obligation that is built on phallic reproductive sexuality. In this respect, Freud was a fundamentalist too. He couldn't shrug off the weight of social and religious tradition that prescribed women's place, so instead he misdescribed our bodies—an error from which culture is only just recovering.

Desire

IN HIGH SCHOOL, MY FRIENDS and I whispered about the physics teacher who touched girls' breasts. We knew girls he had done it to. Ick, Mr. *Tindley!* He was middle-aged and mousey but had a knowing twinkle behind his eyeglasses.

Like adolescents everywhere, we felt our daily condition veer from chronic sexual arousal to humiliation and terror. None of the adults in our lives acknowledged the desires that drove us—certainly not our parents, and not the other teachers, Miss MacEachern with her prim Latin mustache, nor Mr. Gutmestadt who kept a bottle of whiskey in the file drawer of his algebra desk, nor even Miss Keane, who wore chic suits and taught biology—except Mr. Tindley, and he was icky.

Arousal

Our bodies embarrassed us by their excesses and deficiencies; our uneven breasts, our oily skins. In freshman year many girls were dealing with sanitary napkins (tampons were a little racy), but menarche still loomed for some of us, one of many hurdles in our paths. The boys sprouted pimples, hair, strange odors, and occasional erections that made us giggle or blush.

And we giggled about Mr. Tindley. None of us ever admitted desiring him, but he promised access to the mysterious world into which our bodies were hurtling us. An ordinary little man, he twinkled with some promise, some juicy knowledge. His sexual presence protruded into physics classes and study halls. We had no sense that he might be in our power—that we might exploit his weakness—only that he could lead us somewhere we had never been, his flute a glass pipette, his cloven feet hidden inside his wingtip oxfords.

I never had a class with him, but forty years later I remember him as part of my sexual coming-of-age. How many of us had a Mr. Tindley, a teacher, baby-sitter, uncle or aunt, a janitor, a stranger, who by words and looks and sometimes touch erupted into our lives with disturbing force because his lust (or hers) chimed with our secret wishes? I know now that some girls were truly harassed by him and suffered; some ignored his intrusion; but some of us yielded, at least in thought. The physics teacher's ickiness annealed itself to my sexual feelings, and I knew I was not alone.

He wasn't the first person in my life to link erotic promise with danger and humiliation, but he came at a crucial time. Feminist theorist Judith Arcana says, "Terrible things happen to women under patriarchy." They happen to men, too. Adults treat babies' little bodies as sexual toys or jokes. Parents touch them, tease them, pose them for photographs, and believe they won't remember the things that happen to them before they can speak. You would think adults would know better. Early psychoanalytic literature is filled with case studies of patients who, as children, were licked by big dogs or had their hands tied by their nursemaids. In later life, these patients became aroused by the sight of a dog on the street or a pair of handcuffs dangling at a policeman's belt.

Our hopeful, desiring bodies arrive into a world of others who were touched and teased as babies, grown-ups for whom eros is linked forever to feelings of shame and anger. Every pinch, every flash, every dirty joke strengthens the chain of association, until it's nearly a miracle that lovers can ever be truthful or kind to each other—because the one thing we have in common seems to be shame. No wonder we stare into mirrors, desiring the other who might be just like us, whose perfect understanding could suspend the chain. No wonder we fantasy perfect partners, silent partners who will spare us the humiliation of speaking our desire, of asking for what we want.

Some people are able to move beyond shame in their sexual-expressive lives, but some can't. And almost universally, feelings of sexual desire and the physical changes of arousal are chorded with feelings of loathing, anger, guilt, or fear. For some, the positive experiences of pleasure and love have buried those ancient layers of anger and shame, like the luminous nacre that covers a piece of grit and buffers the pain it causes to an oyster. But for some, sexual expression remains rageful, painful, corrosive — a dire thing. These are the people who become the sexual criminals, abusers, and monsters we spin fantasies about.

In Roberto Benigni's comic film, *Il Mostro,* the ostensible joke is that the gentle hero—who gets himself into clumsy predicaments with knives and chainsaws—is mistaken for a rapist murderer who is terrorizing Rome. The real joke, and the real horror, is that stories of the murderer's crimes arouse pleasure and desire in the police, in newspaper readers, in the hero himself, and of course in the viewers of the film.

The object of this "comic" violent sexual fantasy is usually a woman's bleeding body. (American filmmakers have begun to show equal-opportunity mayhem in horror films, perhaps egged on by "Joe Bob Briggs," the late-night TV horror-movie host whose comments always include indexes of dismemberment.) Some female viewers will be repelled by the fantasy, but some will respond to it with shudders of fascination and pleasure, gazing at women as objects of lust—that is, desire for pleasure mixed with rage.

The first object of desire for most infants is the mother's body; it is the paradise from which we are expelled, our first lack, and the rage that is tied to desire is rage at the mother's body. We're all born, and we all share in this tie; it's this rage that lets us laugh at "comedies" like *Il Mostro.* And because we all know the rage, we understand what impels some humans to wreak sexual torments on others.

Many women are completely turned off by these

fantasies but some, like me, disapprove of them yet can't help responding pleasurably. Women, as feminist philosophers note, live on this cusp of desire: We experience lust as culture has written it in us, desire bound to rage, yet vast numbers of us have had the rage of others turned against our own bodies. We have been raped, beaten, tortured, humiliated, and insulted by those who claim to love us, beginning with our families. Enormous numbers of women have been victimized by men—or women—who are aroused by violence, and the pain of that experience can overpower their own infantile desire for revenge on the maternal body. Some women who have been victimized succeed in recovering from their wounds. Some join the oppressors' club. For some, pain dissolves the complicated weave of displacement and masochistic pleasure that makes up much of feminine sexuality, and they reject sexual expression altogether.

The paradox—that desire leads us to express our deepest love sexually, and yet our sexuality is tied to violent self-loathing—has led some writers, like Konrad Lorenz and Robert Stoller, to conclude that sexuality *is* essentially aggressive and violent, and that rape and sexualized murder are just fucking well inevitable. But I'm trying to clear another path for desire.

A young girl sits alone in a room, in a straight-backed chair, her back to the door. It is a summer evening. Window shades are drawn against the day's heat but soft sounds can be heard: children's voices, a dog's bark, the clicking trills of birds and insects. She wears a white

Arousal

peasant blouse, with elastic drawn through the neck; it can be pulled down over her shoulders, and this is what she has done. She expects something. She smells her own clean sweat and feels the rise and fall of her breath.

A young boy enters the room. She doesn't turn. He walks up behind her and puts his hands on her bare shoulders. His hands feel hard and dry, and they are hot. She smells the dull male graphite odor of his sweat. Her heart beats fast. She doesn't speak. He doesn't speak. She wants him to reach into the drawn neck of her blouse and fondle her breasts. She got the word *fondle* from a book, and it excites her. She has anticipated this moment for weeks. But he doesn't do what she wants; he brushes the outside of her blouse with hasty hands and runs out of the room.

She has anticipated this moment for weeks. The words for what she wants are "feeling up," and the boy's name is Kenny Bloomfield. "I'm dying for Kenny Bloomfield to feel me up," is what she told her friend Dalia. Dalia boasts that she has been felt up. She also boasts that she is friends with Kenny, a lovely, baddish boy. Dalia agrees to get Kenny to come and feel her friend up, but we can't risk discovery. We have to find a time when someone's parents will be gone. Dalia says Kenny will only do it if she can be there, but I say she has to wait in another room. Now I don't know what I'm feeling. It was over so fast. Did he really feel me up? I know he didn't do what I had in mind. I wanted him to give me pleasure, and to take pleasure in giving it.

That girl in the peasant blouse was not a beauty, not a flirt, but she was trying to stay in control of her life. Her body teased and thrilled her with promises of arousal, and a sense of awakening interest on the part of boys she knew led her to imagine that one's touch would deepen her feelings. She wasn't willing to take her chances with a whole gang of boys, the way hoodie Peggy Breyer did, but she was willing to risk a certain amount of humiliation, because Kenny might tell. Dalia (though pledged to silence) might tell. Perhaps she sensed that selecting a lover to pleasure her wasn't wholly dishonorable.

Why did Kenny agree, and then why did he refuse? The role of consort didn't come naturally to him. Boys were supposed to take the initiative and press themselves on girls, who were supposed to set limits, deny pleasure, defend themselves. Did it upset him to have the rules changed? Did it occur to him, I wonder, that he was being used?

That scene happened in the summer of my thirteenth year. I didn't yet understand the intricate rules of teen sex, and by the next summer I had lost the lordly innocence that let me design my own scene; arousal had become a weapon to deploy in the war between male and female, and my breasts were territory to defend or yield, strategically. Winning meant dishonor—lying about my own arousal, or damping it—but losing meant defeat by the double standard, alive and well in the fifties, and emotional complexities for which I wasn't ready, like humiliation, independence, and autonomous desire.

Then, when I was fifteen years old, I was in an auto accident. There were six of us in the car, and most of us got banged up somewhat; my date, a smart, gentle football player named Paul, was in a body cast for months.

Arousal

Although I was walking around before Paul, I had been hurt worse: internal injuries, a fractured pelvis, and a concussion that left me first comatose, then delirious, for nearly a month.

I had a big crush on Paul. What a violent word! We only ever kissed, or maybe he put his big, hesitant hand on my breast. But I fantasied about him, and on some level I might have believed that the accident and my injuries were punishment for my desire.

When I woke from the delirium, I was lying in a hospital bed, my hands tied to the rails. Tubes ran from my belly to invisible machines. I itched but couldn't scratch. The nurse who came in looked at me warily, with pursed lips. While delirious, I learned gradually over the next day or two, I had been loudly obscene and abusive to both myself—tearing at the tubes that drained my bladder, ruptured in the crash—and the nursing staff—hurling bedpans, cursing them out with language no one knew I knew. Quite like the little girl in *The Exorcist*. The wary nurse couldn't see at once that the delirium had cleared and I, a reasonably polite teenager, was back.

Maybe the damage of the crash, and the trauma of surgery that my body must have felt as further damage, tightened an association between my lust for Paul and pain. Maybe I began to see sexual encounters as a way of proving that I could feel desire, become aroused, and survive.

I still dreamed of a lover who would give me pleasure on my own terms, but the reality of the boys I knew drove the image far into the future. I thought of these dream lovers as older men, though not Mr. Tindleys—*attractive* older men. Perhaps older men and older women attract us in youth because we imagine they can play the games of sex more freely, more surely. With skill comes the knowledge of when to break the rules; for example, when to let a girl take charge. Also, their faint tarnish arouses us—smudges under their eyes, a loosening of flesh at the jaw line—as Odette's gaunt quattrocento beauty aroused and troubled Swann. We imagine they have spent nights in slow erotic invention, sacrificing sleep to pleasure; we imagine their bodies have been molded by prolonged caresses.

When we come to be fifty, of course, freshness holds the magic; fantasies of inexperience arouse us, taut and trembling youth, eager, dewy, half-afraid. Perhaps when aging women and men look over a roomful of fresh meat, they see themselves; perhaps they imagine correcting the record, going back and doing it right. It takes most of us a long time to welcome desire, and unless we're very lucky, almost everyone's early memories of arousal are laced with shame and regret.

A few years later, I was seventeen and a student in Paris, where I met an older man who advanced my education in pleasure. A struggling actor in his early thirties, Gérard shared a room with a friend, Alys, who worked as hostess in a gay bar. Alys had tried out Gérard when she was freshly divorced, but they didn't please each other as lovers, although they got on well as roommates. She thought she might try lesbian sex, so she had a couple of dates with her *gouine* friends, but they didn't please her, either.

Arousal

Alys would dress for work at six in the evening and come home about four in the morning. I often spent the night with Gérard and usually slept right through Alys's entrance, unless she brought a friend home. We sometimes made love in the mornings while she slept. On Mondays, when the club was dark, Alys cooked amazing dinners on an alcohol stove.

On Sundays, Gérard and I took lunch with a pair of bachelor friends, Claude and Jean-Marc. Alys contemptuously called them *"les hommes de bonne volonté"* because, like the characters in Jules Romains's novels, they were inseparable friends, minor civil servants who would never marry but live out the lives of modest boulevardiers. I called them The Boys.

We met at a shabby, admirable old restaurant, Chez Poussineau on the rue Bonaparte. My companions always asked M. Poussineau what was good that day and usually ate it—brains in black butter, loin of pork with lentils, rabbit stew. M. Poussineau made a special *chou-fleur à la crème*, passed under the *salamandre* long enough to glaze it with delicious dark brown spots; we always ordered one of those for the table, and sometimes two. I loved the sweetbreads, the kidneys, the long-cooked ragouts of veal and hare. Gérard liked to end the meal with a *pot de crème*, but The Boys and I preferred cheese.

Jean-Marc was florid and ample, a good-looking athlete going slightly to seed. Claude was thin and quick, with dark hair that fell into his eyes; he wrote verse, political satire mostly. They both wore mustaches, Jean-Marc's a red-gold walrus and Claude's a dark toothbrush. The

Title:

Arousal : bodies and pleasures / Martha Roth.

Item barcode: 32091025716102

Hold note:

Title:

Arousal : bodies and
pleasures / Martha Roth.

Item barcode: 22091026716102

four of us usually sat at a table in the back room, where serious regulars in dark jackets and sweaters pulled their bentwood chairs up to the blue-checked tablecloths.

Sometimes Jean-Marc brought a letter from his mistress to share with Claude and Gérard over Sunday lunch. She was a married woman, and they had been seeing each other on free afternoons for years. One letter detailed the clothes she planned to wear for their next meeting and in what order she would remove them. The shoes and stockings were to come last.

"Last?" I asked. "Is that sexy?"

"Oh, yes, yes," they all assured me. "Especially the stockings."

"Really? Will they be black stockings?"

"It doesn't matter," shrugged Jean-Marc.

"I prefer a paler color," said Claude.

"You don't even wear stockings," said Gérard.

"Would you like me to?"

"I like you as you are," he said. I felt young and small, pressing my nose against the window of a house where grown-ups played secret games, until I realized that just as Gérard's age made him appealing to me, my inexperience aroused him. I was not a woman writing on scented paper about her plans for slowly taking off expensive clothes bought by her husband, but a student in pullovers and black tights.

There was a complicated pleasure for us all in having me share the letter. When Jean-Marc next met his mistress, he might add a description of the scene at the lunch table to the activities of the afternoon. When Gérard and I made

Arousal

love, perhaps we performed for an imagined audience of The Boys. Folds of possibility lay about us, like extra widths of heavy satin in the skirt of a ballgown, light burnishing the belly of a fold and leaving its crease in darkness. If Claude's sensuality was—as Gérard and I thought—solitary, we could only imagine what roles we played in his private theater, where audience and performer might be the same. Did Alys really sleep through our morning loving, and did my desire for Gérard include a sense of her presence?

Jean-Marc's leisurely layering of anticipation and remembrance showed me something new as he exhibited himself and his lover for his mates' pleasure. Perhaps my being there added a little kick, like a pinch of cayenne pepper in Poussineau's sauce. Later he could squeeze some more juice from the memory by evoking it for her, lapping it over onto itself like a roulade. Each repetition would reflect all the others, like mirrors placed to copy images into infinity, except that here each reflection changed the original, deepening and enriching its sensual value with new wrappings.

One could extend arousal forward and back in time, rolling it into narrative and stretching it to cover erotic affection for one's friends. It could hide in plain sight until a later touch or word released its fragrance. I was far from ready to admit that I was sensually attracted to a woman, but I liked Alys, her cooking, her frankness, her slightly passé designer clothes, the touch of her olive-skinned hands, her perfume, her husky voice.

Desire

The agreeable sounds of the restaurant—voices, the clink of glassware and of cutlery—its light and warmth, the mingled scents of food and of patrons, were already a part of Jean-Marc's next afternoon meeting with his lover. Part of what made my dish of braised kidneys wonderful was their hint of urine, transformed and enhanced by skillful cooking. The *civet de lièvre* retained the rank flavor of wild game. "Do you remember that December afternoon chez Poussineau—?"

My mother's mouth was large and busy. She was a wonderful cook, and mouth pleasure mattered in our household: entertaining talk, good food, cigarettes, whiskey. Certain words—as when she said that someone was "rich as Croesus"—made her mouth water and deepened her voice, as though they were delicious. My saliva would flow, too, when I was a little girl.

I remember the intense pleasure of making certain sounds: *dja dja dja, ye ye ye ye.* Flattening my tongue and pressing the syllables out through a narrowed mouth sweetened them and made them into little pillows of deep grief and joy. The feeling gripped me, spoke through me. Language didn't have enough of those lovely meaty sounds, and I needed to make them; I would be miserable if I didn't say *"Lililili gyung gyung gyung gyung,"* working teeth and tongue and palate right then in just that way. In kindergarten I knew a beautiful little boy with white skin; I dreamed of biting him—not to hurt him, exactly, but to mark his whiteness with my desiring mouth. From such

Arousal

secret knowledge I began to understand that love and anger ride in our mouths before we speak them; we want to bite and suck what we love.

When my friends and I were at the stage of whispering and wondering about the great mystery of sex, the idea of French kissing and "frenching," as a word for genital licking and sucking, disgusted and fascinated us. The first taste of someone else's tongue was shocking, but the shock faded rapidly and the fascination persisted. A few years later came the delights of eating and being eaten.

After we are born, the first thing we love is the nipple in our mouth, the breast or the bottle, and every later love awakens this fierce urge. Perhaps it also awakens the rage we felt when breast or bottle was empty or taken away. Freud used the term *oral aggression* to describe the wish to bite and chew someone we desire. The wish, in the end, to eat them.

Everyone has these wishes, though few of us ever act on them beyond the odd passionate bite. You can't really eat people, as Flanders and Swann cheerily reminded us; it's the ultimate taboo, stronger than incest or murder. When this taboo is breached by a psychopath in Milwaukee or a soccer team stranded in the Andes, cultural attention zooms in and dwells with fascination on the event, the crime, the phenomenon of people actually eating people.

Othello aroused Desdemona wth his tales of "anthropophagi." During centuries of exploration and colonization, travelers from industrializing countries had a first question they asked any tribal people: "Do you eat human flesh?" As if cannibalism would justify whatever the colonizers wanted to do. Christian, Muslim, and Jewish slavers used the presumption of cannibalism—along with "paganism"—to justify their enslavement of millions of people in the Americas and Africa.

The arousing, disturbing fantasy of cannibalism turns up in all sorts of scientific inquiry, travelers' narratives, anthropological studies, even in the work of Charles Sherrington, "father of modern neurology." Sherrington extended Charles Darwin's work on the emotional expression of animals by removing parts of animals' brains or cutting through their spinal cords without killing them; he was trying to localize different aspects of their behavior in the remaining parts of the brain.

I have trouble with the image of grown men flaying and mutilating turtles, frogs, and dogs to see whether their emotional expression is located in their brain cortex or elsewhere, although there's a horrid *Dr. Moreau*-ish pleasure in it, too. Sherrington's work prepared the way for later research on brain and spinal-cord function, yet he was a vivisectionist, one of those creepy figures from the sentimental books about dogs that my friends and I read when we were ten or eleven. In Albert Payson Terhune's books, a shadowy villain always lurked, waiting to trap his canine heroes and sell them to scientific laboratories.

I first read Sherrington's papers in a college biology course when I was eighteen, eons away from the sentimentality of *Lad, a Dog* and susceptible to the cold, impersonal thrill of science. To summarize his findings on canine cannibalism, in many tries Sherrington couldn't induce a laboratory spinal-cord-transected dog to eat dog flesh, but one

Arousal

of his colleagues successfully coaxed a pet dog with an intact spinal cord to eat some. Sherrington concluded that dogs have an "instinctual" inhibition against eating their own kind, but they can overcome it for love.

The interesting question is why Sherrington was so interested in dog "cannibalism" that he structured careful experiments to investigate it. When tribal people include the eating of human flesh in their customs, it seems to be highly ritualistic, like the eating of communion wafers that one believes to be the actual body of Christ. When the human being eaten represents an enemy, the sharing of flesh may be an attempt to incorporate the enemy's powers, or to assimilate the invader. But in Western fantasy, the literal eating of human flesh seems to represent an outer limit of sensuality. Was Sherrington investigating an erotic fantasy?

One might believe that French culture, so frank and inventive that we called oral sex by its name, acknowledging multiple pleasures and flooding ordinary life with erotic energy, would have no room for images of violence, coercion, or pain. Au contraire. Many deeply French writers, the marquis de Sade and Georges Bataille among them, are virtuosos of imagined erotic torture and cannibalism. As though the more civilized and commonplace mouth pleasures were a zone that must be crossed on the way to monstrosity, outrage, death. How is it that all of life's luck and sweetness can't transform the core of rage and shame on which culture winds its scroll of sexuality?

Living in France taught me another lesson as well. As a Jewish woman, I was a certain kind of sexual object to Frenchmen. When I described myself once as *"une juive,"* literally a female Jew, I embarrassed Gérard, who hastened to assure me I was an *"israélite."* Such words as *juive, négresse,* or *tonkinoise* carry a sexualized charge, turning a woman into the representative of an exotic conquered, enslaved people—like the phrases "Black girl," "Spanish girl," or "Indian maiden" in the United States. Like the Jewish spies or prisoners I pretended to be in front of the mirror, the women of a people bear with them through time the erotic burden of abominable acts, and this consciousness can sharpen "normal" sadistic or masochistic fantasies of sex between people of different colors or nations.

Such loathsome desires can strike an echo in the sexual image reservoir, the way Mr. Tindley's reputation as a molester echoed my adolescent fantasies. Why should torture, cannibalism, or slavery be described by pornographers as refinements of pleasure, and why should we ever desire them? They have to do not with pleasure but with our need to confine and punish our eros, our mute, helpless, pleasure-seeking selves.

Silence

THE MOTIF OF THE SILENT WOMAN crops up in folk tales of many cultures. Silence is sometimes a curse laid upon a young woman who must do extraordinary labor before she can regain her voice. Or sometimes a virtuous man is rewarded by having his wife fall silent. Or a king's daughter is born voiceless and begins to speak only when a visiting prince agrees to marry her. Rabelais and Ben Jonson played with the motif of the Silent Woman, as did Anatole France.

Then there is the Silenced Woman, her tongue cut out so that she cannot tell what has been done to her, like the mythic Philomela, whom the gods changed into a nightingale, or Shakespeare's Lavinia, daughter of Titus Andronicus.

Arousal

Most statues of goddesses that have survived antiquity have lost their heads, along with other parts. All statues of course are silent, but headlessness calls attention to their silence, especially since these female figures have strong bodies and sometimes powerful wings. If their arms are still attached, they may hold weapons. These headless figures have exerted a strong charm on the modern imagination, which I think is probably due in part to their underlined or redoubled silence, and painters and sculptors have imitated their mutilated form. The Silent Woman is a woman who cannot speak for herself or say what she wants.

In a thoroughly nonclassical contemporary version of the figure, the artist Robert Crumb, in Terry Zwigoff's documentary film, *Crumb,* talks about one of his best-known comics, "Bitchin' Bod." Mr. Natural comes to visit Flakey Foont, bringing with him a live, voluptuous, headless woman wearing a bikini. "Here," says Mr. Natural to his friend Flakey. "She's yours."

Flakey—a weedy gent who resembles the artist—is spooked at first, anxious and uneasy at his headless prize. Mr. Natural shows him the little cover over her neck, like a teapot lid; it comes off, but it's neater to keep it on. Mr. Natural leaves. Flakey looks at the figure with a mixture of fear and lust. Lust wins out as her bulging breasts and thighs attract him more than her headlessness repels him, and he positions her for intercourse. "Here's where I start to get excited," says Robert Crumb.

Watching the film, I start to get excited, too, although I am appalled at the image, and it occurs to me that the anxiety and nausea I'm feeling may be ordinary accompaniments to arousal, for Crumb and for millions of other people, male and female.

Flakey fucks her from behind, and it's "the best sex" he's ever had. But after some plot twists, Mr. Natural must rescue Flakey from accusations that he is responsible for this woman's headlessness. Mr. Natural takes off the lid on the woman's neck and reaching down inside, in what Crumb says his wife calls "the most disturbing" panel, pulls out her head by the tongue. "You mean it was there all the time?" says Flakey. "Sure," says Mr. Natural. "Don't tell her."

Reassembled, she turns out to be Devil Girl, a stock Crumb character whose voluptuous body and filthy temper express the cartoonist's own special blend of sexuality and terror. She rages at Flakey and Mr. Natural, screaming, "I'm going to cut both your heads off!"

Critics have described Crumb as an artist peculiarly of his time. His fantasy about a headless woman seems to me to express a triple wish: (1) to maim a desirable woman; (2) to have a desirable partner who is silent; and (3) to have his desire and pleasure, his arousal, construed as a misdeed or even a crime, perhaps because he feels so guilty about both (1) and (2). In order for him to have pleasure with her, she must be radically silenced—beheaded—and he must be punished for these twin wishes (for pleasure and for cruelty); he must pay for sexual pleasure with humiliation and pain. The fulfillment of (3) comes when Devil Girl threatens to cut off both their heads—Flakey's and Mr. Natural's, the brain and the penis.

Arousal

There's more: intercourse, a pleasure for Flakey, insults the woman. His penis degrades her, and she craves revenge. Her name is Devil Girl. The devil is a woman. The devil made me do it. You made me love you. Let's do it.

At nine and ten, I liked to play with the McNultys, who lived in the building over Kleins' shop and went to parochial school. They said the priests lectured the boys about impure thoughts and told them that girls are "near occasions of sin." The nuns told the girls they were that, too. "The devil finds work for idle hands," they said, meaning masturbation. At least the McNultys knew they had bodies and desires; like me, they knew that certain pleasures were exciting and forbidden, exciting *because* forbidden. Their teachers teased them with the flames of hell. I just wanted to grow up.

Crumb needs to round out his excitement with punishment, but his need has curdled my excitement. My response has been contradictory: the image of the woman's body and the man's desire excited me, but the headlessness combines with Flakey's punishment to short-circuit my arousal, and it evaporates. I'm acutely aware that he has drawn a sexually potent woman and then reduced her to a headless doll with a lubricated opening, like an inflatable *dame de voyage,* who can't really play with Flakey or express her own desire for pleasure.

This feels familiar, and I realize that many times my arousal has followed this pattern: A man's fantasy first arouses me with images of his arousal and then turns me off because it has no space for my pleasure or my desire. For too many men, it seems, the sexually desirable woman is a silent woman, a silenced woman—at least partly because a voiceless woman can't deny or counter a man's fantasy that her pleasure exactly mirrors his.

A rhetoric of women's specific erotic pleasure is missing in this Crumb comic, but then, it's missing from most of culture. The speechless lubricated passage, the vagina, represents women's sexuality in story, song, myth, joke, painting, and sculpture, and while vaginas are undeniably important, they are not the center of specific female arousal and pleasure. The tiny, potent clitoris is; but the clitoris is mainly unrepresented in art or literature. Looking for traces of its presence becomes a real snipe hunt: it isn't there, *ça n'existe pas.*

Women as represented in art and—until the revolutionary work of Masters and Johnson—science have no independent principle of sexual arousal. They are purely responsive creatures. Even the mythical condition "nymphomania," a pseudoscientific term meaning "insatiable sexual desire on the part of a woman," takes its name from the labia (nymphae) of the vulva rather than from the clitoris.

Human Sexual Response, the massive volume in which Dr. William Masters and Virginia Johnson published the results of years of experimental research with volunteers, began to shift the cultural edifice built on women's silence. As more women write books and make art, and as various silences on the subjects of pleasure are broken, the cultural image reservoir is becoming more abundant and inclusive, but the clitoral presence is long overdue. Seventy years ago Gertrude Stein included a coy discourse of clitoral pleasure

Arousal

in works like *Tender Buttons*. Twenty-five years ago poet Muriel Rukeyser wrote:

> *In the human cities, never again to*
> *despise the backside . . .*
> . . . .
> *In the body's ghetto*
> *never to go despising the asshole . . .*
> . . . .
> *Never to despise*
> *the clitoris in her least speech.*

Thirty years ago novelist Monique Wittig's lyrical prose works, *Les Guerrillères* and *Le Corps lesbien,* began to build a new symbolic structure for women based in accurate physiology. Artist Carolee Schneemann's photographs of her own body from the sixties are, she claims, the first representations of the female nude to feature "a visible clitoris."

Certainly, Gustave Courbet's explicit nineteenth-century female nudes, including his famous "L'Origine du monde," shock us today more by what they don't show than by what they do. Courbet manages to focus on the naked female groin without representing its precious details. That is, he paints an absence, a fantasy of the body part that is the "origin" of men's pleasure, and omits women's.

In the 1960s, French critic Guy Hocquenghem wrote of the "silencing of the anus," and gay male writers on sexuality who followed him have discovered that their voices, too, remain unheard; except for *Naked Lunch* and some of Robert Mapplethorpe's photos, there are few mainstream representations of the anus as a center of erotic pleasure. I'll hazard that the silence of majority culture surrounding clitoris and anus has taught women and gay men either to lie about their sexuality or to remain silent. Women's bodies have been written over by male lovers with the text of their own pleasure, and this accounts for the persistent lure of the fantasy of the silent lover, the "obscure" object of desire.

Women's arousal can be invisible to men, and because most women don't look at their own vulvas in an aroused state, we don't know how to show them. Men want to look at the vulva, are fascinated by it, but can't "see" it; what they see is a holder for the penis, not a cluster of different organs, each responsive in a different way and each a source of pleasure. Irigaray's *This Sex Which Is Not One* refers to the lips of the vulva as multiple organs, not one, and never counted in theories of female sexuality. As she says in her essay "Blind Spot of an Old Dream of Symmetry," in her book *Speculum of the Other Woman*,

> *The pleasure gained from touching, caressing, parting the lips and vulva simply does not exist for Freud, he is unaware of it or prefers not to know about it. At this stage or any other. Just as he will never refer to the pleasure associated with the sensitivity of the posterior wall of the vagina, the breasts, or the neck of the womb. All organs, no doubt, that lack masculine parameters?*

Arousal

The vagina feels like the most important organ to men because it holds their most important organ. Our sexual folklore and our literature, art, and films describe and demonstrate a kind of sexual mirror play in which the movement of the penis in the vagina arouses a woman exactly as it arouses a man, even though *Human Sexual Response* gave scientific proof that it is vibration of the clitoral hood that arouses the vagina, and that the fingers, lips, and tongue do this better than either the penis or the flat pelvis.

The folklore of romantic love has constructed women as liars, faithless and secretive. Sex is a slippery business, as others have remarked before, and when a woman is making love, she is usually not keeping track of the clinical stages of her arousal. But however fond she is of a lover's penis, and however exciting various kinds of penetration may be for her, her pleasure center remains the little clitoris that has the Latin name of *membrum muliebrum,* "female member." Still, because the language and imagery she sees and hears trumpet her vagina as her center of erotic pleasure, she makes some private accommodation, agreeing to behave like the woman constructed by culture and reserving to herself the truth about her body that this construction leaves out. Is this concealment? Is it lying? Since the coming of the sky gods, women have survived in culture by keeping silent about misrepresentations of their bodies.

Some books on sex feature cross-sectional diagrams of the clitoris, showing how its anatomy resembles that of the penis, with its bulbs and caverns, its spongy tissue and rich circulation. The physiology is similar, too, because the

Silence

clitoris becomes engorged much like the penis, and some women claim that it ejaculates—though unlike the penis, a urethra doesn't run through it. But the clitoris has a fantastic number of nerve endings for its size, most of them extending from the pelvic plexus, whereas the vagina has comparatively few.

The vagina occupies its privileged position in culture because it first receives the penis in intercourse and then becomes the birth canal. In fact, the vagina has two entrances, one from inside the body, hidden from ordinary view, and one from outside. Sexual folklore seethes with anxious images of the depth and mystery of that opening into the body, and how dangerous it is for the fragile wand of the penis to enter.

What goes *in* is men's terror and pride; what comes *out* is either garbage—discharged semen, blood-stained cotton—or treasure: a baby. We are all born, in St. Augustine's resonant formula, *inter faeces et urinam,* "between shit and piss." A twentieth-cenury version:

Q: How do we know God isn't an engineer?
A: Look at how he runs a sewer right through a playground.

Screams

Deeply held convictions powered my early sexual activity, but I'm not sure where I got them, from John Stuart Mill or Lenin's friend, Clara Zetkin, or from my parents' cautious bohemianism. I believed a woman had the same

Arousal

right to sexual passion as she did to intellectual freedom, and she had the right to choose and change her lovers. Our biology must never be our destiny.

I shed virginity when I was fifteen, after drinking a lot of gin. I don't remember much about the first time except that it hurt, but by the second time intercourse stopped hurting and began feeling good. I decided I liked it, although the pleasure I felt was quite distinct from the pleasure of masturbation and never even began to approach a climax.

Still, there was a whole new world of subtle sensation to explore and—since my pleasure had no crest and no particular dynamic, an easy beginning and no real end—I could go on for hours. I had many partners, back in the carefree 1950s, without much emotional commitment, although of course I preferred some boys to others—they were more graceful, more playful, smelled better, lasted longer. I was in love with some of them for a couple of months.

Most boys didn't know much about sexual anatomy, and I wasn't going to tell them. My clitoris belonged to what I still believed was "immature" pleasure, and I was hell-bent on maturity. If a lover tried to lick or stroke my real center of pleasure, I discouraged him. "I don't need that," I said, impatient to get back to fucking, which I was sure would one day produce ecstasy. It was *supposed* to. All sorts of authorities said it did: Freud, Havelock Ellis, all the marriage manuals. More important to me, D. H. Lawrence, Ernest Hemingway, and even Mary McCarthy said, or implied, that it did.

Most young men subscribed to the same sexual mythology, and I found several boyfriends who were into long, meditative couplings. I became a screamer. Pleasantly drugged by our rhythmic rocking, the kissing and thrusting and rolling, the fresh moisture of our shared fluids, I would begin to groan a little, working up to a full-throated moan. Then my breath would catch and I would yelp. If we went on long enough, I would be panting and howling. Sometimes my partner would shush me, embarrassed.

There was a lot of exhibitionism in these performances, which were certainly meant to be overheard. But the screaming wasn't wholly intentional; it seemed to just happen, at a certain point. It wasn't exactly a trance state, either, although my concentration was profound. The vocalization expressed what I wouldn't allow myself to feel; I think I was giving voice to my silenced clitoris.

When my best friend ended her virginity, she said tentatively (because this was in 1955, before much open discussion of bodies or pleasures, and she'd read the same books I had), "It's sort of a transfer of sensation, isn't it?" and I said, "O yes, yes it is." She and I both believed that with the right partners, fucking could somehow reengineer us, hooking up the sensations that reliably produced pleasure to different parts of our bodies.

We had, as Irigaray points out in "Blind Spot of an Old Dream of Symmetry," no language or culture for describing our own pleasure. So although we were acquiring new repertoires of feeling in and on our beautifully foliated bodies, the language of our sexuality had been written for us by men, men whose imaginations and powers of

Arousal

observation were limited by the same false sexual ideology that assumes that desire and pleasure, arousal and climax, are phenomena based in male bodies. And women had gone along with this charade. We had no words for our real feelings or fantasies; in my case, at least, they were too bound by shame because I hadn't yet had the "right kind" of sexual pleasure.

My friend was less tense and ideological than I, and soon an experienced lover helped her to full arousal and orgasms. But even with clever, attentive lovers like Gérard, I didn't want to have the "wrong" kind of pleasure. I'd bought Freud's version cock, cooze, and clinkers, as you might say, and for a few years I waited for a miracle that never happened.

At my first job, as editorial drudge in the office of a medical journal, I had to check footnotes. In the course of research in the medical library, I came across some of the papers that Masters and Johnson had begun to publish in the late fifties in the *Western Journal of Obstetrics and Gynecology*. It's fascinating to me that I had to read about it first, but their published research, their text, gave me permission to trust my body and begin making love. I found a tender, patient lover who seemed pleased to learn about my vulva and used his tongue and his fingers to caress my clitoris, and I stopped screaming. My body began to claim what it knew, in silence and in speech, about pleasure.

But not without conflict. Masters and Johnson were only two investigators. Could the entire weight of psychoanalytic theory and practice be—wrong? All the marriage manuals, all the novels? Evidence lay close at hand, but ideology pulled me in a contrary direction.

During this season of intellectual doubt and ecstatic lovemaking, I had a dinner-table conversation with a handsome uncle whom I adored, my father's youngest brother, who was a psychoanalyst. Uncle Randall had gone to medical school and then into the naval medical corps; when I was a small child, he was a dashing lieutenant. After the war he took psychoanalytic training, and in the late fifties he was living in New York and practicing as a by-the-book Freudian analyst. (He was later booted out of the New York Institute for Psychoanalysis—because, among other reasons, he refused to see patients for fewer than the canonical five sessions per week.)

Randall was thorny and provocative in his personal relations, and his sarcasm scared but intrigued me. I'd had erotic fantasies about him when I was younger, and whenever he came to Chicago to visit my parents, I was eager to see him. My mother made a bouillabaisse, and we were drinking wine. Randall had recently separated from his first wife, an actress, and he talked about her rather bitterly. "She could never accept her femininity," he said.

I had read enough of Freud to understand this coded statement; I was just coming into my own sexual power; and I'd had a glass or two of wine. Freud's notions about mature female sexuality, and thus about healthy femininity, might be wrongly founded, I said, because there were few or no nerve endings in the vagina.

Randall put down his spoon and stared at me. "Oh, really? How do you know?" he asked. Then he picked up

Arousal

his napkin and wiped his lips. His blue eyes sparkled, squeezed by a big smile. "How many vaginas have you dissected?"

The best-known writer on women's sexuality, Sigmund Freud, famously believed that human sexual development mirrors the Oedipus myth: Men desire their mothers and want to kill their fathers, and guilt over these desires makes them anxious about their penises. Women, on the other hand, desire their fathers and hate their mothers because they have no penises, and they can only find fulfillment in bearing and suckling children—mainly sons. Women are stamped from early childhood with desire for a penis and anxiety over its lack. Freud related almost everything his patients told him, everything he heard or thought about women's sexuality, to what he called their castration.

In the last twenty years, feminist writers like Julia Kristeva, Gayatri Spivak, and Luce Irigaray have shown that although castration may not describe women's psychosexual development, it amounts to an ideological position that describes how men see female sexuality. It also keeps them from any clearer or truer understanding of women's real sexual differences from men. In language and in cultural imagery, women are the *lacking* gender, the ones without.

Jacques Lacan has helped to advance this delicate discourse by his gloomy view of men's sexuality: He uses the word *phallus* to mean not an erect penis but the concept of "the father's" potency, which men as well as women lack. In a lecture at the Collège de France in the late 1980s, when asked what was the truth about sexuality, Lacan said, *"Il n'y a qu'une seule vérité: la castration* [Castration is the only truth]."

Irigaray's essay, "Blind Spot of an Old Dream of Symmetry," comes from her book *Speculum of the Other Woman*. The old dream, of course, is the wishful fiction that women's bodies and pleasures should be exactly reciprocal to men's—mirror images, as Freud believed they were when he decreed that "mature femininity" involves a "transfer of sensation." When a woman fully accepts her femininity, he wrote, then the "immature" pleasure a child finds in her clitoris will mysteriously give way to mature, that is, vaginal, feeling.

It sounds impossible, and it is. Freud never pretended to understand it, though he insisted (as did his faithful disciple, my uncle Randall) that it was true. In Freud's day, of course, accepting femininity meant a great deal more than the loss of clitoral feeling; a woman who made the "mature" choice to marry also accepted a husband's domination, corsets, compulsory childbearing, and silence.

This "blind spot" or scotoma must be exactly the same size as the clitoris. It must be fitted to it, tight as a contact lens, because—like the opaque rectangles that blank out the eyes of people in tabloid photographs—it masks the fountainhead of female arousal and pleasure while locating it precisely. This tiny organ, which holds so much meaning for women's sensuous life, beginning in infancy, is—as Virginia Woolf said of women in general—"all but absent from history."

Arousal

Why should a scientist as eager and intelligent as Freud insist that clitoral pleasure is "immature"? Why should he describe vaginal pleasure as "authentic," superior? Why, because the vagina receives the penis, of course, and the penis is—the penis is—what *is* the penis, that it should deafen scientists (who have it) to evidence and cause them to misrepresent reality to their women patients (who don't)?

Castration is the only truth.

Penis Envy

Freud broke amazing ground in his research and thinking about human psychology. But because he ignored women's precise experience of arousal and fulfillment, the imagery and language of sexual love has continued to be almost entirely a dialogue of penis and vagina. The old dream was of a totally mirrored, reciprocal sexuality, like a young man's fantasy: "Is it good for you, too?" The old dream was that intercourse—an enjoyable arrangement for men—automatically pleases women, and if it doesn't, this must be because a woman suffers from penis envy, the pathological desire to have a phallus (not in the Lacanian sense) of her own.

Women do have phalluses of our own, of course, small but perfectly adequate as pleasure centers. That fact—that women have phalluses, and that our sexuality is always at least partly phallic—seems to have scared Freud into consigning the clitoris to the pitiable shadow of immaturity. Rather than acknowledging that male and female are more alike than different, and that gender consists more of behavior than biology, Freud held strict views of sexual polarity. For a woman, the only "mature," acceptable fulfillment for her penis envy is a baby, preferably a son.

Woody Allen, in *Zelig*, says, "I broke with Freud over the question of penis envy. He wanted to confine it to women." Thanks to the work of such French Freudians as Lacan, Cixous, and Irigaray, it's now clear that anxiety about male organs—their size, their presence, and the possibility of their loss—belongs mainly to men. Irigaray suggests that the indispensable Freudian diagnosis of penis envy might be an artifact, created by the analyst to explain anything he doesn't understand about his women patients' sexuality. And how can he understand them when his science is built upon their silence?

> *... what she [a female patient] comes to say while in analysis will not be very different from what she is expected to say there. And if she didn't say it there, why should she bother to come? To this scene that is organized, also, by/for her 'penis-envy.' And what could an analyst make of a desire of hers that would not correspond to his* wish? *For the penis. He would be, Freud confides in us, quite helpless.*

After my brother's birth (when I was six), my mother became depressed. She stopped working at her job so that she could stay home with the baby. She felt tired all the time and neglected her appearance. The baby was troublesome; he spit up, squalled, and had allergies. She had

Arousal

difficulty nursing him. All his rhythms and features seemed strange to her, whereas mine, presumably, had been familiar; but then, I was a girl.

She went into analysis, which was what a lot of women of her class did at the time, and—it makes perfect sense—discovered her own penis envy. After she had been in treatment for a year or so, my father began psychoanalysis with a famous old émigré doctor who had been analyzed by Freud. This was in the forties, when the Institute for Psychoanalysis recommended that spouses be treated to help them handle changes in their partners' psychic adjustment.

My parents felt a messianic enthusiasm about the insights they were gaining as analysands, and they thought it would be a wonderful idea to make these insights available in plain language. They decided to write a book for young children called *Psychoanalysis and You*. Because they had a little home laboratory simmering with sibling rivalry, they used me, age eight or nine, as a laboratory specimen.

Their first step was to explain that I was unhappy because I suffered from penis envy. Probed and prodded by these affectionate amateurs, I retreated into guilty silence. Of course I hated my brother, but not because he had a penis; I had been a precocious only child, the center of their attention, and he displaced me.

But it must have been easier for me to go with this cover story than to face—and talk about—the towering rage I felt toward the baby. On weekends, my mother and father worked on the book, cutting into the time either one might have spent with me. I couldn't bring up my own problems, when theirs hung in the air of our apartment like the blue layers of smoke from their cigarettes.

My mother's unhappiness is easier to understand now, after the feminist movement of the 1970s. Suddenly bereft of an interesting job and colleagues she loved, confined to the society of a sullen six-year-old and an infant, and believing that her unhappiness proved she was not accepting her proper social and biological role, how could she be happy? And how could she break her silence, except with the words that were prescribed for her?

On most nights of the week, during the years my parents were in analysis, only one of them would be home for dinner with me and the odious baby brother, sometimes mother and sometimes father. We ate in the kitchen, at an enameled tin table with painted legs, under the harsh light of a naked bulb, not at the polished wood table in the lamplit dining room. I felt my parents had abandoned me, one at a time, and I certainly wanted something, but I don't think it was a penis.

My parents sent a proposal for *Psychoanalysis and You* to agents and publishers, but no one seemed interested, and after a year or so they dropped the project. My mother finished her analysis. My father abandoned his. My brother and I reached a stage of armed and fragile truce.

If women envy men, we can now see that it's because of the privileges their anatomy confers and not the anatomy itself. Many of Freud's women colleagues disagreed from the beginning with his rococo theories of female sexuality,

Arousal

but the weight of analytic opinion stayed with the men. Freud called psychoanalysis "the talking cure." Our parents' experience with it drove me into silence. I began to understand that even beloved authorities weren't going to speak accurately for me, and, further, that silence can imply consent.

Cruelty

FREUD, WHO THOUGHT AND WROTE so much and so anxiously about sexual relationships, believed that every lover focuses not on the actual beloved but on a mental image that he called the introjected presence. Writing at about the same time, the novelist Marcel Proust expressed a similar idea more gracefully in *Within a Budding Grove,* the second volume of *Remembrance of Things Past:* "No doubt very few people understand the purely subjective nature of the phenomenon that we call love, or how it creates, so to speak, a fresh, a third, a supplementary person, distinct from the person whom the world knows by the same name, a person most of whose constituent elements are derived from ourself, the lover." In other words, what we love, at least in the throes of

Arousal

romantic passion—the subject of popular songs and lyric poetry—is not another person but a wish, a desire. The lover imagines a beloved who will be her/his missing half, a mirror image and a complement.

Although I believe with Freud that all sexual pleasure involves some kind of narrative fantasy, I also believe that in intimate relationships, most people try to escape this house of mirrors. We agree to behave as though our lovers were real to us—as real as they are to themselves. In our sexual expression, we engage in a mutual agreement to go beyond self-pleasuring; more, we delight in giving pleasure. Even if we're hip enough to mock the ecstasies of romantic novels, shared pleasure seems a goal worth reaching for. We may not always achieve it; we may struggle, in our erotic imaginations, with childish assumptions and violent fantasies; we may not even try hard all the time. But in committed relationships, most of us do try.

I can't use the vocabulary of love to describe the others, the ones who don't even try. Some people's experiences have been so brutal and demeaning as to sour them permanently on sexual tenderness. Many have been betrayed by the adults who should have nurtured them. Some rapists belong in this second group, as do all of those whose sexual fantasy narratives deny the possibility of the other person. Because other people have no meaning for them, they are truly prisoners of their fantasies, and their sexual interest is aroused mainly by images and fantasies of bodies being dominated or harmed.

Such people represent one extreme of human experience, yet somehow we all can understand their extremity, as though its seeds, or its shadow, existed in us. Cruel and violent images and stories are so much a part of what we call "sexuality" that we don't even question them.

Sex-and-violence, although deplored by parents, pacifists, and religious Muslims, Jews, and Christians, is fed without respite to everyone who watches movies or TV or who reads comic books or the novels of Tom Clancy or Danielle Steel or who sees ads in magazines or on billboards or at bus stops. It is fed as well to anyone who reads the literature of the past or present, Homer, Aeschylus, Euripides, Virgil, Dante, Shakespeare, Daniel Defoe, Victor Hugo, Charles Dickens, Ernest Hemingway, William Faulkner, Thomas Pynchon. Anyone who looks at the painting and sculpture of the past sees violence eroticized in the powerful bodies of horses and men wearing loincloths or snug metal clothing, and sex shown as violent in the many representations of rapes, mutilations, and murders based on classical and biblical sources. A look at modern or contemporary art yields repeated images of women's bodies displayed as though they were fruits or vegetables in a grocery case, to be bought and consumed without the least hint of mutuality.

In this culture we identify cruelty as a sexual pleasure and sex-and-violence as twin springs from a single source, well said in the little phallic rhyme with which, according to Stanley Kubrick's film *Full Metal Jacket,* Marine Corps recruits are drilled: "This is my rifle, this [*hand on penis*] is my gun; This [*rifle*] is for fighting, this [*penis*] is for fun." The story we tell about male desire includes the desire to harm, to crush, to explode, to kill. Is sexual arousal

Arousal

always shot through with cruelty to the point where we tacitly understand that desire pushes men toward murder? The men who learn this rhyme aren't supposed to be at the extreme pole of lovelessness. They're supposed to be good men, men able to love and care for others. I guess they're supposed to be able to switch off the notion that their bodies are weapons.

Or maybe not. Maybe that notion is just part of sexuality. Maybe their wives and girlfriends are aroused by imagining lethal weapons inserted in their vaginas, in their mouths. Women lust; our desire is also mingled with rage because we are born and have the same early experiences of love, hate, and split consciousness as men; but we don't imagine our bodies as weapons in the same way. Our primary sexual organs don't protrude; they are tucked into folds of flesh and bone, and most of us discover them as zones of feeling rather than as feared-for, separable parts.

Some women, discouraged from touching themselves in childhood, don't discover their pleasure centers until they are grown. Some women who have been severely abused or terrorized grow up in such a state of alienation from their bodies that they never do.

The mutilation of women's genitals is the most extreme form I know of denial of specific female pleasure. A worldwide movement to end this cruel practice now involves hundreds of thousands of women and men. The excisers, the people who actually cut out young girls' clitorises, are women who themselves were excised in their youth—a horribly concrete image of how women pass along to later generations the sexual violence that

Cruelty

is done to us. Many women who have seen *Warrior Marks,* the film by Pratibha Parmar and Alice Walker, talk about the glassy, glittering eyes of the exciser who tells the filmmakers that the mutilation is done for reasons of "cleanliness." The logical ground for this belief must be that desire and pleasure—on the part of a woman—are filthy.

Most women in the United States feel safe from genital mutilation, but we inherit silence and pass it on. Later, we absorb the multiple messages that our vaginas are fascinating and terrible and that no other parts of our vulvas exist.

Culture doesn't give women our own script or set of images for independent sexual arousal and pleasure; until recently, the only script we learned was a mirror response to men's. We're supposed to turn the rage in our lust against ourselves, our own bodies. Culture conscripts us to fight for the other side, against our own safety, well-being, and pleasure.

Among my early memories is an innocent, deliberate torture—innocent because I remember feeling no guilt or shame, or rather, I remember a slide from innocence to guilty pleasure. I was about five, and a little neighbor boy and I were dropping his kitten from the back porch railing of our apartment house to see if it would land on its feet. My family had just moved into the building. I was wearing a yellow sunsuit appliquéd with a design of flowers and a watering can.

I don't remember whose idea it was to drop-test the

Arousal

kitten, but it was a lot of fun. The kitten squealed and struggled a little, and it did always manage to land feet first. We climbed the back stairs until we reached the second story, then the third. We didn't think what might happen if the kitten *didn't* land on its feet. We ran downstairs and fetched it after each drop—it must have been dazed, to let itself be caught—and hurried up, our hearts racing, to drop it again. It was a hot day, and we were sweating, panting, and happy.

I don't have any question about where our pleasure came from: tyranny in its purest form. Small children begin life as helpless subjects. We live in a world of thwartings, of smacked hands and bottoms and loud sharp voices, dominated by large bosses and praised for being obedient and submissive. *Naturally* my little friend and I enjoyed dominating a fluffy, adorable creature that was weaker than us.

Some parent stopped us from further tormenting the kitten. We weren't punished but we were shamed, and my mother forced me to acknowledge exactly what we had been doing. My mother disliked cats, I knew, and she wasn't shaming me for harming the animal—as far as I could see, it wasn't harmed at all. She was shaming me for my excited pleasure, and that afternoon was the last time I could enjoy cruelty without guilt.

Not long after the kitten episode, that little boy and his family moved away. His father was a physicist, one of the many who came to work on the Manhattan Project at the University of Chicago. Several apartments in our brown brick six-flat building housed children whose fathers turned out later to have been working on the bomb; a couple of them have won Nobel prizes. In 1943, of course, this tremendous violence was still potential—a terrific secret, and well kept.

Another memory of innocent pleasure turning sour: A slightly older boy named Gib lived in the next building. He had red curls and a disdainful laugh, and I thought he was wonderful. He teased and taunted girls, and he only played with me once, when we spent a whole afternoon hugging and kissing and rolling around on the linoleum-covered floor of my bedroom. I must have been six. I remember it as bliss, and I was eager for more. From being a bully and a wicked object of fascination he had become a tender lover—a transformation, I later found, that organizes a lot of women's sexual fantasies.

I don't know how Gib's mother found out what we'd been doing, but he was never allowed to play with me again. What's more, she treated me as though I'd done something naughty. My mother and father didn't punish me, but they said what we'd been doing wasn't a good idea. Why, I wanted to know; it felt so good. It just isn't, they said, embarrassed. Gib ignored me after that, slowly breaking my heart.

Later that same year, there was a sensational murder case in our neighborhood. I was just beginning to be able to read for myself. An undergraduate at the University of Chicago abducted, murdered, and dismembered a little girl of about my age. Every evening's paper carried the

Arousal

news of another brown-paper package discovered in a drain, containing yet another piece of the child's body. I had trouble sleeping. I didn't want my window open (the murderer had climbed in the girl's bedroom window), and I couldn't breathe in the muggy summer nights when it was closed.

My parents told me the things one tells a child—there are people so sick and confused that they want to hurt others—but the crime struck some chord of murderous lust in my six-year-old soul, and I knew there was more to it than that. Night after night I masturbated until I was worn out and could sleep. I don't know whether my guilty terrors aroused me or whether I was simply comforting myself, but I was so shamed by the chiming of my own desire and pleasure with this monstrosity that I couldn't tell anyone. Now I think the depth of my fear had to do with my wish to kill my baby brother—the wish that our parents had enthusiastically explained as "really" a wish for his little button of a penis. The nightly terrors and the dreams that woke me from exhausted sleep were the punishment I dealt myself.

A couple of years later, in a book called *A Child's History of the World,* I first saw respectable printed confirmation that cruelty is enjoyable. In a chapter called "Kings with Corkscrew Curls," the author, a prep-school history teacher, wrote with considerable relish and gratuitous homophobia about the Assyrian kings of Nineveh:

> *... you may think that only girls wear long curls and that a man with curls would be 'girl-like.' But*

Cruelty

these kings were not at all that kind. They were such terrible fighters that they were feared far and near. They treated their prisoners terribly; they skinned them alive, cut off their ears, pulled out their tongues, bored sticks into their eyes, then bragged about it.

I understood as any child would that a writer who goes into such detail is having a good time. These extremes of cruelty thrilled me, too, not wholly unpleasantly, and they put the dismemberment of a single child into a horrible context. It was a relief to think of that dreadful crime as *not so bad*.

    These kings had resonant, mysterious names: Sennacherib, Assurbanipal. We lived near Breasted Hall, home of the Oriental Institute of the University of Chicago, a museum of archaeology where finds from Tutankhamun's tomb were permanently displayed along with replicas of other booty from digs in the Middle East. There was a copy of the Rosetta stone, which held out the tantalizing offer of cracking another code, another system of reading, and there was a set of galleries with Assyrian statues—bull-headed gods and lions with men's faces, awesome, gigantic sculptures. I often visited these galleries, which usually stood empty, and I worshipped the enormous monsters with furtive devotions, saying the strange names over to myself. Their size and power aroused me and once I masturbated in front of the bull. Was the author of the *Child's History* aroused by their power as well—was that the source of his pleasure?

Arousal

Evil and Danger

A classified ad in the personals column "Women Seeking Men" asks for "long-haired, evil-looking guys." Another ad says, "Must look evil."

By *evil* these women probably don't mean Bertrand Russell's poverty, disease, and corruption; they probably mean something funky and knowing, something close to the blues, to Horace Silver's "Filthy McNasty." *Nasty* describes a good guitar lick; *bad* means fine-looking and effective. *Evil* means sexy, as opposed to the blandness of *good*. Girl Scout cookies are *good,* and family movies about dogs. Goodness has been cooked too long. Evil is fresh.

"Lactating pregnant biker bitch," reads an ad in a pornographic magazine. "Went to gangbang, got knocked up, need big strong daddy to keep me in line." Probably a professional sex worker placed this ad, but who will answer it? Some man who finds the fantasy appealing. Because of the complicated texture of desire, even forty years into the sexual revolution, for many men women are still divided into nice girls and sluts, the clean dull ones you marry and the hot babes who excite you: Virgin and Magdalen, mother and whore. Because she arouses his feelings, the desirable woman is a figure of danger to a man.

Danger is thrilling, and glamour is dangerous; the movies have given us all fantasies of the wicked woman, the sleek temptress who drains men and discards them, and of the vampire, the serial killer whose love is mixed with deadliness. The Lorelei attracts plenty of sailors, and

Bluebeard never stays single for long. Sylvia Plath wrote, "Every woman adores a Fascist, / The boot in the face, the brute / Brute heart of a brute like you." Women write letters to men on death row who have raped and killed other women; they send their photographs and pieces of their underwear. Ordinary women who feel drawn to their extremity, aroused by it, offer sex, marriage, money.

Maybe a woman tells herself that something else is arousing her: he's in trouble; she has a chance to save him. Maybe she tells herself that what is aroused in her isn't lust but pity; she is drawn to a man who has done dreadful things because she can save his tormented soul by the force of her love. He murders people or blows up buildings because he has never known the transforming power of passion like hers.

It would be too simple to say, primly, that a woman who offers her body and her money to violent, criminal men suffers from low self-esteem. Or that because she comes from an abusive family, she's drawn to men who will mistreat her. But one could say that her sensuality has been constructed in a certain way. What arouses her, what she thinks of as sexy, is close to what's dangerous, even lethal. What draws her is the explosion, the murder, the blood and suffering, because a connection has been made in her, too, between pleasure and cruelty; she, too, has old associations of pleasure with forbiddenness, violence, and power. Crime arouses her.

Goodness may be an exciting idea morally or philosophically, but sexually it's boring, even though we know that the qualities of a good lover—tenderness, patience,

Arousal

generosity—are more likely to be found in a good person. Still, many women cling to the fantasy of a rake whose sexual force will sweep them along. In real life, a man who disregards his partner is likely to rape her. In fantasy, a greedy intensity may arouse us where tenderness doesn't. We mistake brutality for playful spontaneity.

Such fantasies have created a billion-dollar global market in romance novels. As described by sociologist Janice Radway, in *Reading the Romance,* the genre has many subcategories, from formulas that begin with outright abduction or imprisonment to dreamier, *Jane Eyre*-like plots, to novels that are hardly distinguishable from mainstream fiction. Some of the categories are historical, with one whole subgenre set in the Regency period in Britain. Others are geographical: castles on rocky coasts are favored, and many plots take place in Cornwall or Normandy (alternative settings for *Tristan and Yseult,* one of the greatest love-death scenarios). A woman who has little concept of her own autonomous sexuality and few images for female pleasure imagines a partner who will do it all for her, whose arousal and climax will produce, or coerce, hers. In romances, of course, the hero gentles under the heroine's influence, and they live happily thereafter.

The male inflection of the romance fantasy is a little different: The arousing woman is a perfectly satisfying sexual partner, but the hero's survival depends on leaving her or killing her. Occasionally, as in the Lorelei story or in contemporary versions like *Fatal Attraction* or *The Last Seduction,* the arousing woman intends to harm her lover(s), but more often her wickedness consists of having had several lovers, or having survived by selling sexual access to her body. Her crime is her sexuality. In Romantic versions of the story, like *Manon Lescaut* or *La Dame aux camélias,* the hero may be threatened with loss of class or income. Sometimes the threat is to the hero's line of descent, either because the arousing woman has a different "racial" heritage or because she has had many lovers (and presumably cannot be trusted to remain physically faithful to the hero). Sometimes the arousing woman is a criminal, like the Gypsy Carmen.

In men's imaginations, the sexually independent woman is both arousing and dangerous. Surely that's what nineties fashion is about, tight black leather clothes, navy-blue fingernails, blood-red lips. In women's romantic fantasies, the alluring partner changes from a threat to a protector. In men's fantasies, they protect themselves: the alluring partner must die, or at least she must be abandoned.

There still aren't enough good stories about sexy women who are both desirable and desiring and who survive the last page, the last act, or the final reel. Where, in our puritanical culture, can young people find images of independent female sexual pleasure? Their mothers flutter in a web of responsibilities to others, whether they work outside the home or not: to children, husbands or boyfriends, parents and siblings, employers, teachers and principals, bureaucrats. Independent sexual pleasure isn't usually high on the list. The only single women most young girls know about who aren't pining for marriage are nuns, and they submit—gladly, we're told—to a rule as

Arousal

stringent as any faced by a poor wife barefoot, pregnant, chained to the stove.

Lesbians model an authentic, female-centered sexuality, but even in the era of k.d. lang and Melissa Etheridge, homophobic laws and customs make it difficult for many young women to see lesbian love as an option for them. Because lesbian sexuality threatens social arrangements, and despite the growing acceptance of lesbian households, woman-loving women are both mocked and demonized in popular culture. The ironies of compulsory heterosexuality insure that in terms of images in the popular media, the only woman who is represented to the eyes of the impressionable young as both enjoying sexual pleasure and controlling her own life is a commodified woman—an actress or model posing seductively, displaying her body as though it were for sale.

These actresses and advertising models supply so many of our images of sexual allure that they have come to define it, and women aren't perceived as sexual beings unless they are seductively posed; unless they are in some way acting like whores. Actresses and models learn whorish behavior and poses, and advertising art becomes pornography, in its old Greek sense of "writings and drawings of whores," because it shows women displaying themselves like merchandise. For young girls, the intimate sense of physical pleasure, the knowledge older than language, old as the nervous system, that we bring with us from infancy into childhood, becomes annealed to our dawning notions of commodity. Young boys see these same images and learn as well that women's sexuality is something they will

Cruelty

be able to buy. The warm thrill of sexual arousal becomes something to exploit, a card to trade.

We really did trade cards, playing cards, when I was in fourth and fifth grade, but only the girls. Starting with jokers scrounged from our parents' decks, we built up collections of fifty to a hundred cards, trading two, three, or four less valued backs for one beauty. "Bicycle" cards were on the bottom, then abstract designs. The more color and intricacy, the more value, although even the gorgeous paisleys weren't as valuable as the next category, landscapes.

Some landscapes were crudely printed and boring, but some had a Hudson River School dreaminess. Then came reproductions of famous paintings (I remember a nice "Blue Boy"), then animals (cats, dogs, and horses, in ascending order), and then the softly painted bodies of women—"girls," we called them—Petty girls and Varga girls. Petty girls posed smiling in pert outfits, and Varga girls pouted naked or wearing filmy lingerie, and both kinds had bodies as anatomically improbable as Barbie dolls: legs three times as long as their torsos, tiny feet and hands, big puffy breasts and buttocks, teentsy waists. When we showed each other our collections, our packs of trading cards, we began with the ordinary cards and led up to the treasures, the women's bodies, both signs of value and valuable in themselves.

These were erotic images in the forties. They seem quaint now, innocent of any suggestion of violence or pain. We might hide our Varga girls from our parents, but if they found them, they weren't horrified. If I write the

Arousal

words *erotic imagery* now, what comes to mind—the pop singer Madonna, wearing leather or tight black underwear? Cranach's Venus, with her small high breasts and jeweled snood? A sultry boy with a big cock poking out of his open fly? To my eye, these all suggest restraint—not emotional restraint, because they're all images intended to arouse desire, but bondage. The boy's flesh strains at his clothes. Venus's hair is bound, her throat and ears chained and pierced by jewels. Madonna overflows the top of her leather bustier. What we currently think of as "erotic" clothing almost always implies a subtle violence: bulging muscles straining at taut uniforms; soft flesh restrained in tight fabric; lace or elastic printing angry marks on breasts and thighs; stiff boots or strapped shoes; precious gems and metals wrought into chains, ropes, straps, or cuffs. Cutting into the body has become an erotic sign: light etching, as in tattoos, piercings, scarifications.

Pain and Blood

In Juzo Itami's film *Tampopo,* a comedy set in a Tokyo noodle shop, two lovers softly pass a whole raw egg from mouth to mouth without breaking the yolk. Then someone bites someone, and their next kiss has blood in it. When I saw the film, this combination of delicacy and violence took my breath away and I thought, *that would be good,* like sprinkling balsamic vinegar on raspberries, a new way of seasoning something. The taste for blood is probably easy to cultivate.

Cruelty

In myth and art, blood belongs to the fierce old matriarchal religions. Blood flows in childbed. Blood is the precious fluid that women shed every month, with no wound. Blood, says Irigaray, is life itself, more precious than semen, more precious than water, and she believes that the importance of blood in sadomasochistic sexual practices stands for the "return" of this primitive value.

Since the advent of AIDS, blood has taken on an even more dangerous allure as the risk of HIV transmission through body fluids has added to blood's magical potency. But blood is dangerous in fact as well as fantasy, and another fluid must stand in for it: both Irigaray and Barthes make a metaphorical comparison of blood with ink. Ink, source of the safest sexual pleasure, circulates freely. Reading and writing, the permitted transgressions, allow us to frolic in this fluid. One of the pleasures of the text, according to Barthes, is that "the writer is someone who plays with [the] mother's body . . . in order to glorify it, embellish it, or in order to dismember it, to take it to the limit of what can be known about the body. . . ."

Arousal to pleasure opens our senses, and many of us find pleasure in pain, dealing it and suffering it. Even gentle lovers trade nips or scratches. Who knows what fantasies flow through people's minds—the bound hostage, masked terrorist, high-heeled dominatrix, shiny-booted officer with a riding crop, the tortured kitten, the helpless prisoner writhing in his/her bonds?

Sexual subcultures—gay, lesbian, bisexual, and straight—have developed kinds of sexual play that don't

Arousal

involve the exchange of body fluids. To make up for this deprivation, people reach for a stronger jolt of fantasy, the old pleasure of cruelty. Much of this play is in the area of sadomasochism, or S/M, ranging from games where we trade the roles of top and bottom, master and slave, through physical stimulation and torture to piercings and penetrations that we can carry on under "safe," clean conditions.

Two lovers go to a party. One has forbidden the other to speak a certain word, perhaps to speak at all. Their eyes meet through the crowd, and they feel the power of connection. They have solved the problem of ennui; nothing is trivial because they have added an extra dimension to their lives. The bottom flushes pink with the pleasure of the top's attention.

Two lovers sit at a café table. One of them wears a little sex toy in the rectum. Their shared secret arouses them. They have drinks, they trade glances, they talk with other friends, but their secret knowledge heightens and burnishes everything. They are performing a scene, behaving ordinarily while linked by an extraordinary relation. Perhaps their arousal will build throughout the evening and further lovemaking will crown it. Or perhaps the concealment and performance are enough.

In private places other games are played, with words, with costumes, needles, knives, whips, or brands. A woman has a rose tattooed on her inner thigh, where only her lovers may see it (and her showermates at the health club). A man wears genital jewelry to give his lovers pleasure, the discovery of gold wires through his foreskin.

Cruelty

Giving pain is an old pleasure. Many children experiment with bullying and torment, as my little friend and I did with his kitten, and most are conditioned away from it, as we were. Some people learn to find pleasure in receiving pain, perhaps in childhood from parents or caregivers whose only physical intimacy is in the dealing of pain. In almost any group of children there will be some who misbehave for the sake of the attention it garners. Some children pick fights in which they are certain to be hurt. I remember a girl at summer camp who sewed patterns in the sole of her foot with black thread and a needle.

A friend who taught first grade told me of a little boy who needed extra attention. One day she asked him for a hug; after the hug, he turned his back to her and said, "Spank me now."

"His mother was a very buttoned-up sort of lady," my friend said, "and I imagine the only time he got real feeling from her was when she spanked him." Maybe it was the only time he was allowed to press his body against hers as well. Poet and novelist Linda Hogan says, "For some [men], the only connection to [their own] inner world has been violence. It is why so many men have described times of war as times when they felt the most alive. It is through events of war that they are thrown into the powerful world of bodily feeling."

For many people, men and women, spanking is a highly arousing form of foreplay. Spanking, birching, caning, whipping, and more serious and potentially damaging forms of "discipline" are very popular. Brothel wisdom holds that the more power a man wields in his life, the

Arousal

more he craves paddling. British men especially seem prone to nursery fantasies, their erotic scene design a cozy mix of *Mary Poppins, Peter Pan,* and Dotheboys Hall from *Nicholas Nickleby.*

American men who don't have a tradition of corporal punishment at school or a children's literature full of nursemaids and mild abuse are forced to generate punishment scenes out of their own image reservoirs; so a Robert Crumb can knit a fantasy like "Bitchin' Bod" out of the pure materials of lust and guilt. His fantasies reach us in comic books printed in the ink that Barthes and Irigaray compare to the mother's blood.

Death

The biblical Rachel cried, "Give me no more children, or else I die." Did it add a mordant twist to Jacob's desire for her—knowing that his love could have lethal consequences?

A man once told me about a woman whose breasts were beautiful "until I got through with them," as though by making love to her body, he had used her up. Humbert Humbert used up his nymphet stepdaughter Lolita, one of the last literary heroines to die in childbirth, evoking the male fantasy that penetrating a woman is wounding her. A trip through an old cemetery supplies plenty of evidence that men did use up their wives, but I'm interested in fantasy, not history.

The notion of giving pain or damage to a lover seems to be deeply arousing to some men. Maria Irene Fornés includes a Spanish joke as an epigraph to her play, *Fefu and*

Her Friends: Two men sit together at a bullfight. One tells the other about his new sweetheart; he praises the woman's beauty and delicate breeding, then says, "And she is here! My love is here today, sitting across the ring."

"Where?" says his friend, peering at the mass of people. "I can't see her."

The first man takes out a gun and shoots at a woman in the crowd. "There," he says. "The one that fell."

I can only fathom this as the revenge fantasy of someone who feels weak and small—a man doomed to fear women because they make him feel like a child. The other end of this story, I think, is the male fantasy that a lover's embrace harms them.

A famous series of Renaissance paintings shows Venus and Mars in an intimate encounter, the naked war god sprawled in exhaustion, for the moment slain by the love goddess. It pleases me to think of love as stronger than war, and I can see how a man might call his orgasm a little death. I can even see that on some deep level of imagination, sexual arousal might be laced with terror. Men's lovemaking involves symbolic physical risk and loss, the entrusting of a treasured body part to another and the spilling of body fluid; nevertheless, for most of history, the consequences of heterosexual love have been much more dangerous for women.

It would take another book to unpick the matted carpet of love and death. Such a book would look calmly at men's hatred and fear of women. Then it would gently take up men's desire for intimate contact with other men and the terror this desire provokes in them. Such a book

Arousal

would include mythic versions of male fear and male love (Cronos and Saturn, as fathers who eat their own children; tragic buddies like Damon and Pythias or Achilles and Patroclus), analyses of myth, and images of the vagina as a seething cauldron or foul cesspit.

Such a book would also take up women's hatred and fear of one another, and it would look at how women's powerlessness in most strata of society, for most of history, has confined them to the home. Then it would probe the many ways women's anger, fear, and jealousy have seeped into our household practices, especially childrearing, so that we have managed to produce generation after generation of women and men who replicate almost the same unbalanced relationships.

Women's mortal terror of men has a sounder basis in fact than men's terror of women, considering the history of women's death in childbirth and at the hands of their lovers. Proust's Swann admired the Oriental despot Mahomet II, who had grown too fond of his favorite wife; he could think of nothing but her, and to free himself of this preoccupation he stabbed her to death. Women as well as men write books and make art in which death figures as an ultimate pleasure, completing arousal.

A modern Scheherezade, the lucky consort who escaped death because she was such a good storyteller, is Dominique Aury, the woman who says she wrote *The Story of O* under the name "Pauline Réage." Her story is complicated (and her real name is not Dominique Aury): She was a single woman with a much older lover, and what she prolonged from day to day with episodes of her story was his sexual interest, his actual arousal. Scheherezade spun stories that kept her master interested, incomplete stories with fascinating characters and events that left him hanging, always wanting more, so that although he had condemned her to death, he could not bear to have her killed. She stayed alive from one day to the next by keeping his curiosity aroused.

The life Aury was saving was the life of a love affair, the intimacy and juice between her and her lover that had been the emotional center of her life. Without his fantasy investment in the story of O, her lover would have been just another impotent old man and she an aging woman; because she spun for him a fantastic tale of cruelty and desire, they could remain lovers.

When I read it, in 1967, *The Story of O* aroused and horrified me, calling to secret terrors and pleasures remembered from childhood, although I was not a child but a young mother nursing a baby. I pretended to read *Histoire d'O* as a philosophical exercise. Parroting the publisher's blurb, I told myself it wasn't "just" pornography but the story of a spiritual quest, the story of a woman who is broken to the discipline of absolute submission.

I was sure a man had written it, a clever man with a Jesuit education, because the heroine's fate parodies Christian martyrdom. I didn't yet understand that, as Susan Griffin says, "The metaphysics of Christianity and the metaphysics of pornography are the same."

Classically, pornography subverts religion by turning its symbols inside out, and this inversion of orthodoxy is one reason why pornographers, in the United States at

Arousal

least, attract support from fervent believers in free speech and the separation of church and state. I was certain the author was a man because of the peculiar sexual physics of the text: O locates her sexual response in her belly, and the book's most vivid images are of piercing and insertion—for example, O must wear in her anus a graduated series of obelisks made of semiprecious stone. No one gets wet in *Story of O;* it's a dry dream of artifice and attitude. I thought: a man's fantasy.

But in 1994, the author came forward. *Histoire d'O* was written by a woman who understood that a fantasy of victimization and terror would arouse her aging lover, particularly when she gussied it up with religious and philosophical trappings. Aury, with an experienced woman's grasp of classical pornographic imagery, wove a fantasy of abject sexual slavery.

In the last chapter, O appears naked, a chain passed through her labia, wearing an owl mask and presiding over the torment of a young woman friend. At the end, O goes to her death, a death presented in the novel as freely chosen—and, in the strict tradition of Romantic pornography, fit punishment for an arousing woman.

In an earlier tradition, the owl is a bird sacred to Athena or Minerva, the Greek or Roman goddess of wisdom and childbirth. In Celtic lore, the owl is associated with the Crone, the woman who can no longer conceive children, third aspect of the Triple Goddess. Owls were also called night-hags, associating them with the daughters of Lilith, the succubi who teased men's semen from them in sleep, creating—according to Hebrew mythology—

demons. So the symbolic flavor of the owl mask is strongly independent, indicating perhaps that O has indeed chosen her fate, or perhaps that the teller herself can choose another. Dominique Aury, the woman who says she wrote *Story of O*, manipulated her lover's arousal with a fable of masochism and subordination. Perhaps she wreathed her heroine in owl feathers to signal her own freedom from the thrall in which she netted him, her refusal of O's fate.

A long time ago I had a lover who was a doctor in a provincial English city. His daily tasks were the ordinary ones of a general practitioner, delivering babies, dressing wounds, treating chronic diseases, and dispensing drugs. One night as we sat late over supper, he told me he had helped his uncle Jim to die.

"You've heard of Brompton mixture," he said softly, trimming ash from his cigar. "Jim had lung cancer. He didn't want the end to go on and on, and he asked if I'd help him out."

Out. I'd heard of Brompton mixture, or Brompton Cocktail, as it was sometimes called, developed at Brompton Hospital to ease the pain of dying cancer patients. The cocktail contains a lot of heroin, and some other things, and it's supposed to smooth the transition from life to death, making it not just painless but pleasurable.

This was the first I knew that my lover had killed someone. He had adored his uncle Jim, and he had helped to kill him lovingly, as an act of mercy, but coolly. It had pleased him to give the sick old man a last experience of pleasure.

Arousal

We sat over coffee and brandy, and I heard rustling wings.

"He trusted you," I said. I couldn't take my eyes from his.

"Yes. It went quite smoothly. You give it three times, you know, for pain relief. . . ." He smoked and looked away.

"And then it kills you."

"Yes."

After a moment I asked, "How did you feel about it?"

"What, about helping Jim to die? Quite good, actually. Margaret thanked me, you know. It made it all easier for her."

Quite good, actually. What exquisite foreplay. I was becoming aroused. "You could kill me," I murmured, "I mean if I were ill, or something. If you had to." It was only partly a question.

He gazed into my eyes. "Yes," he said.

My wonderful lover. My angel of death.

Considering the weight of cultural evidence, there should be no mystery about why some women find victimhood, or fantasies of victimization, arousing, at least some of the time; the mystery is why we all don't locate our sexuality, all of the time, in pain and destruction.

Fantasies of Fertility

A WOMAN SILENTLY RECEIVES the valiant penis and its seeds. Silently her body processes this raw material into an infant, and nine months later her once receptive vagina disgorges a being that will displace her lover from her breasts and bed, a being that might—like Edmund, like Oedipus, like Zeus himself— grow up to harm or kill its father.

In the past thirty years or so, writings by women scientists, critics, philosophers, and poets have so radically changed the way we think about gender that it's difficult to remember how recently most of women's energies and desires were routinely suppressed. Women entered business or politics only as appendages of their husbands or fathers. Quite intelligent people believed that women could not be

Arousal

great scientists or artists (let alone fighter pilots or astronauts) because our creativity supposedly finds expression in conceiving and bearing children. Almost no one believed that a woman could have a full sexual life and a family *and* achieve professional distinction.

Yet even as barriers against women began to fall in one profession after another, the truth about our sexuality still was denied. The most thorough investigators seemed to have trouble accepting women's abundance, our capacity for independent pleasure *as well as* the mysterious gift of fertility. Well before the 1997 cloning of Dolly the sheep, successful parthenogenetic reproduction of newts and other amphibians led some feminists to jeer that human males need to claim sexual superiority because they are biologically less important.

Male "birth" is a staple of science fiction, from Mary Shelley's *Frankenstein* to the *Alien* series, where men—virile American men—are impregnated by a repulsive reptilian entity that is the extraterrestrial being. When the product of the pregnancy emerges ("is born"), the men are destroyed. Take away the postmodern glitter and grunge of the scene design, and this story echoes the fate that for centuries befell twenty to forty percent of women: death in childbirth.

For all the scholarship lavished on early modern comedies like *Much Ado about Nothing* or *Taming of the Shrew,* in which the theme of heroines' reluctance to marry is held up, examined, and analyzed, few scholars talk about the real-life hazards for a Renaissance woman of entering the cycle of reproduction—saying goodbye to the companions of her youth and cleaving to a husband, to bear and rear his children. Virginia Woolf famously described the subjection of such a woman in the seventeenth century, passed from a father's authority to a husband's and liable, if she expressed wishes of her own, to be "locked up, beaten, and flung about the room." But even Woolf didn't talk about her risks of dying or being crippled by childbearing, or by a husband's rage.

In folk songs of the "murdered-girl" genre, a young woman's pregnancy frequently appears as a motive for murder by her lover. Studies of domestic abuse have shown that women are more likely to be battered by their partners during pregnancy than at any other identifiable time.

Victorian and Edwardian novels are full of middle-class women with mysterious ailments that keep them confined to a couch or a bedroom, some of them, like Proust's Aunt Léonie or the heroine of *The Yellow Wallpaper*, depressed or neurotic. Feminist scholars have inferred that the recurrent presence of sick women might reflect widespread damage to women's sexual organs, much of it stemming from sexual activity and childbirth: uterine or vaginal prolapse, pelvic inflammatory disease, chronic cystitis, or pelvic-floor collapse, conditions that would have been painful, debilitating, and unmentionable in polite society. Working-class women who suffered from these conditions would have had no choice but to go on working until they died.

In many places in the world, of course, childbirth can still leave women with lasting pain and damage. Men beat women all over the world. Sexually transmitted diseases,

Arousal

especially HIV infections, still harm women's bodies and shorten their lives.

In the First World, however, many women can choose with more or less certainty when their sexual lives will include the chance of conceiving a child, and they run a much lower risk of damage in the process of childbearing. These facts have begun to change the relation of bodies to pleasures, but psychology hasn't yet caught up. Change occurs unevenly, too; most women in the world still risk pregnancy with every act of sexual intercourse. But in the popular culture that the United States exports, pregnancy now appears as a chosen condition.

If worship of a great goddess truly did characterize an ancient phase of human history, evidence indicates that the goddess was worshiped mainly for her fertility and less— if at all—for her prodigious sexual capacity. Although the pleasures of arousal are seen to lead young women straight toward the dangers of pregnancy and childbearing, women's sexual pleasure has always been at least partly separable from the capacity to conceive. Not that there's no connection: for many women and men, fertility is sexy, and the possibility of conception can add to arousal. But in biological terms, clitoral pleasure has no function beyond itself; it is "excessive."

In the early 1970s, I worked in a sort of contemporary temple for the worship of genitalia: a department of obstetrics and gynecology in a university medical school. My boss was a surgeon with wide interests: infertility, contraception, abortion, and human sexuality, as it was called, to distinguish it, I supposed, from teacup or toadstool sexuality. I was interested in sexuality, too, and though he had hired me as an editor and writer, he also used me as a lay advisor, a kind of feminist conscience.

One of my jobs was to sort through the dozens of professional journals that came into the office and set aside any that might interest him. One beautiful glossy, called *Medical Aspects of Human Sexuality,* was filled with four-color reproductions of art from East and West, Chinese scroll paintings, Japanese block prints, Persian miniatures, and European paintings from Piero della Francesca up through post-Impressionism, with occasional American pictures for good measure: Andrew Wyeth, Edward Hopper, John Sloan. Some of these were conventionally erotic images but not all, and the art pages had only the most tangential connection to the magazine's contents. The articles dealt with sexual and reproductive functioning: "Effects of Prolonged Insulin Use on Sperm Motility"; "Declining Age at Menarche of American Girls"; "Contraception in Traditional Cultures"; and so forth. Take away the four-color pages and most of the contents could have gone into the various sober professional journals that filled my desk: *International Journal of Obstetrics & Gynecology, Journal of Infertility, Journal of the American College of Obstetrics & Gynecology, Studies in Reproductive Technology,* and the rest.

When I began this reflection on bodies and pleasures, I thought back to that editorial job and tried to remember whether I learned anything about arousal from several years of associating with scientific experts in human sexuality. Its medical aspects, as it turns out, continued and even furthered the tacit effacement of women's real bodies and real experience.

Human sexuality developed as a subfield of gynecology in response to trouble in the discipline. Gynecologists had begun to hear a feminist critique of their practices, particularly their fatherly (or, rarely, motherly) condescension toward patients and their insistence that healthy events in women's lives like menstruation, pregnancy, and menopause needed medical attention and drugs. Challenged, the profession moved in the manner Foucault describes so well in *The Birth of the Clinic* and *The History of Sexuality:* medical doctors annexed territory that had belonged to social psychologists, and they developed Human Sexuality as a clinical field with structures for diagnosis, treatment, and billing.

Although cynics might describe it as a putsch, my boss and his cronies applied themselves to their new subject with a touching blend of innocence and zeal that reminded me of an old boyfriend, a medical student who was the first man who ever went down on me. He had learned about giving head from a lecture that was his school's entire curriculum in Human Sexuality in the fifties. "They told us it's one way to get a woman ready for intercourse," he explained thoughtfully, licking his lips. "They didn't tell us how it tastes."

"How does it taste?" I asked him.

"I don't know. Good."

Heaven knows there are legitimate reasons to teach the medical profession about sexuality. Women have always gone to their doctors for sexual advice, but patients who talk about sexual desire or arousal risk embarrassing their doctors. Women's sexual problems, as distinct from our fertility problems, often concern pleasure or its absence, and far from being sexual sophisticates, most doctors have limited erotic lives. With uncharacteristic insight, my boss described himself and his colleagues as "good obsessive-compulsives"; they tend to be intelligent, driven people who sublimate their desires and defer gratification, and in the 1970s, most of them were still imprisoned in the sexual ideology of the "old dream of symmetry."

Moreover, gynecologists tended to see women's bodies as receptacles or holding tanks on legs. Their specialty supposedly covered our sexual organs but really only recognized their reproductive aspects, and this, too, became a part of the feminist critique. Finally, in the sixties, sexuality along with drugs and rock music erupted into public discourse in a wholly new way. Some medical students and faculty lived with people they weren't married to, grew their hair long, and wore beads. The American College of Obstetricians and Gynecologists (ACOG) tuned in to the possibilities for professional exploitation implicit in sexual liberation.

At the medical school where I worked in the 1970s, all students were required to take an entire course in human sexuality. The language of the curriculum had a distinct masculine bias; arousal was seen as a phallic event, and women's arousal was described as a "response" to that event. (In evolutionary terms, the clitoris is the primary form of the phallus and the penis is a variant, but official language and culture lag behind biology.) Still, they called

Arousal

it "human" sexuality, and I thought I might find some room in it for women's specific experience.

Disappointingly, Human Sexuality focused on outcomes: (1) firm erections leading to (2) ejaculations containing (3) lots of vigorous sperm, landing in (4) vaginas full of friendly fluids that would conduct them to (5) welcoming cervixes and thence into (6) healthy uteri and (7) intact fallopian tubes where they would (8) meet luscious ova and (9) make zygotes that could (10) implant themselves firmly in (11) nurturing uterine walls to (12) emerge forty weeks later as (13) bouncing babies. Oral lovemaking was still considered an hors d'oeuvre.

These outcomes implied orgasms for men but not necessarily for women, whose pleasure lurked at the margins of the new science of "human" sexuality. The work of Masters and Johnson that had so encouraged me a dozen years before *(Human Sexual Response),* and of feminist psychoanalyst Mary Jane Sherfey, whose *Nature and Evolution of Female Sexuality* had a cover illustration of the Willendorf Venus, had begun to influence medical practice, to the extent that steps (4) through (13) were thought to be more likely to occur in the body of a sexually satisfied woman. Still, *a sexual act* was defined in terms of a man's ejaculation rather than a couple's mutual pleasure. (The world was still ten or fifteen years away from Annie Sprinkle's performances. In the film of Annie masturbating to orgasm, fluid gushes from her body in an equal-opportunity freshet that she calls "female ejaculation.") And although the course in human sexuality bravely tackled sexual hygiene for same-sex lovers, the faculty was a lot more comfortable with gay men than with lesbians because at least some of their sexual activity had an identifiable beginning and end.

Some of the newly converted physicians provided sexual counseling services for their patients, and some of the physicians' wives were trained as clinical social workers or psychologists and practiced "couples counseling" along with their husbands. Both men and women patients seemed to resolve their sexual difficulties better when their therapists were a married couple, like Masters and Johnson. "I've got a premature ejaculator who can't hold it for more than thirty seconds," said one hearty physician during a conference planning session. "We've helped his wife learn to climax in thirty seconds, god love her."

The other doctors nodded and murmured congratulations on this feat of sexual tailoring. In my role as consultant I cleared my throat and said, "A woman's sexual response may or may not have anything to do with her husband's ejaculation. Or his erection."

Silence and furrowed brows greeted my remark, then a few nods. "You should be on this conference panel with us," said one of the doctors, but even as he said it, my goal of establishing a beachhead for independent female pleasure receded beyond the horizon. The horizon, for this panel discussion, was reproduction. Pleasure for its own sake might have a kinky interest, but if it wasn't going to affect (4) through (13), the pH of vaginal secretions or the patency of fallopian tubes, it didn't merit a place on the program.

I wanted to know *how* they helped this woman to

Arousal

climax in thirty seconds. When did the thirty-second countdown begin? Did she and her husband prepare in separate dressing rooms, she with a romance novel, he with multiplication tables? Did a bell go off? What, in other words, was her process of arousal?

The doctors were interested in arousal, I knew, because Ob-Gyn, along with other medical and social science departments of the university, sponsored an academic program in human sexuality, which offered a Sexual Attitude Reassessment Seminar, or SARS. The purpose of a SARS was to "desensitize" clinicians to patients' sexual practices or fantasies so they wouldn't faint or call 911 if people talked about unusual acts or desires.

The SARS took place over a weekend, in a large room with carpeting on the walls and pillows on the floor. In this room students, practitioners—doctors, nurses, psychotherapists, clergy—and their significant others watched movies of people having different kinds of sexual relations, and they looked at books and magazines with similar pictures. Then they formed small groups with discussion leaders and talked about what they had seen.

They were expected to be frank about their own sexual lives and to give their partners light massage. Then they watched more films, showing rarer modes of sexual expression, and then they talked about these. The discussion leaders were specially trained social workers and clergy, and the materials ranged from short films of naked pretty people copulating in fields of wildflowers to low-budget, hard-core pornographic movies in which paid actors performed with animals, toys, and one another, singly or in bunches.

Participants were encouraged to wear comfortable clothes—since the only seating was on the large pillows—and to talk honestly about their responses: excitement, rage, revulsion, pity, envy, or boredom. The discussion leaders, I believe, considered any neutral response as a defense, and they "probed" for underlying feelings. Sometimes professional sex workers took part in the SARS as expert consultants. I tried, unsuccessfully, to tell my boss that although prostitutes undoubtedly know a lot about male sexual response, asking a woman about female arousal and pleasure when her livelihood involves faking it is a bit like asking the pope about making mistakes.

Twenty-five years ago the SARS were quite fashionable. Medical schools all over the country offered similar programs, and many students, faculty, and allied professionals went to them, at a cost of about a hundred and fifty dollars a head. They probably succeeded in reducing the shock level of people in the "caring professions," those who look after the physical, mental, and spiritual well-being of others. In my memory the program acquires a wistful poignancy; people were concerned about sexually transmitted diseases in the 1970s, but they meant gonorrhea, herpes, chlamydia, warts. No one had an inkling of how soon doctors, counselors, and their patients would face AIDS.

Many of the SARS materials were pornographic, in its original Greek sense of "writings and drawings of whores,"

Arousal

and all were erotic because they had been created for the purpose of arousing the viewer or listener. But the organizers claimed that the SARS itself was neither pornographic nor erotic; arousal was incidental to the subject of the seminar, which was how to make therapeutic subject matter out of *other people's* arousal. Another aperture for poignancy, here; no one connected with the program, even feminist-conscience me, suspected that the border separating the "objective view" of "caring professionals" who "benefited from" a SARS and the prurient interest of a consumer of commercial pornography might be fragile or porous, or no border at all.

Personal arousal, one's own response, was beside the point. No doubt many of the doctors, nurses, ministers, rabbis, medical students, and social workers sought sexual release in the aftermath of a SARS. They may have hollered, wept, slammed doors, or fought with their partners, but none of that was relevant. It was merely personal, and they were experiencing the SARS as part of their professional development, maintaining a rigorous separation between their feeling, desiring selves—the selves that became aroused—and their judging, performing selves—the selves that counseled others. My boss carried a paperback copy of Xaviera Hollander's *The Happy Hooker* in his briefcase, not for pleasure, he said, but for education. "You can learn a lot from her," he told me, so I read the book. It didn't arouse me, and I never figured out what he learned from it.

In due course, the panel discussion I had helped to organize took place: four obstetrician-gynecologists talking about sexual therapies in the context of marital and fertility counseling. I got to speak as part of a "reactor panel," along with a woman professor of obstetrics and gynecology and two physicians' wives who practiced cocounseling with their husbands. The discussants were all male, we reactors all female.

Women's arousal and climax, I said, might or might not be connected to their husbands' erection and ejaculation. No doubt in many cases it was, but I wanted to be clear that the connection was not automatic. Women's sexuality was autonomous and not strictly keyed to men's.

Silence greeted me. The other women on the panel looked blank. The conference room was chilly (we were in Las Vegas, where it's always cold indoors), but I began to sweat.

"I mean," I said, "there's no *necessary* connection between a woman's sexual arousal or satisfaction and whether or not her husband is potent." I could feel the shovels biting deeper with every word. "That is, the female response cycle is independent of—of—"

The professor coughed. "Of course, there's no necessary connection between full sexual response and fertility, either. Many women respond without conceiving. Many conceive without completing the response cycle."

The physicians' wives relaxed. "The goal of cocounseling is to help the couple achieve the best sexual relationship they're capable of," said one.

The other agreed. "You can't expect perfection."

"It's important to define success for the couple on their own terms," added the first.

Arousal

There were no questions from the audience. Wasn't anybody interested in how women have sexual pleasure? Aren't women human? Women's pleasure may be unnecessary for bearing children, but this panel claimed to be about sexuality. I felt humiliated and out of my depth; I didn't know how to bring in Masters and Johnson's data, or my questions about the thirty-second wonder, or Sherfey's findings of female sexual superiority without sounding like an axe-grinding feminist health freak: "Pay attention to women's arousal! Our bodies are ourselves!"

All the women physicians (not so many), the women students, the therapists, the social workers—didn't they know in their own bodies that a woman's arousal and pleasure can be quite independent from a man's? The SARS and other training must have taught them to ignore their personal experience as "anecdotal," the scientists' strongest word of scorn.

Later, I understood the experience differently. The American College of Obstetrics and Gynecology represented a special corner of the masculine establishment. Women get along in male-dominated society by lying about our sexual reality—or at least by not calling attention to it. No doubt, many heterosexual women find their partners' erections arousing. An erect penis signals desire, and what is more erotic than to be desired? And many women enjoy all sorts of penetration. But I don't believe the official story describes most good heterosexual lovemaking, let alone the large numbers of people who are drawn to same-sex partners or no partner at all.

Although the SARS promised to help in the cultural task of liberating sexuality, its official discourse never broke the silence surrounding women's arousal and pleasure. The only medical condition that can be remedied by helping a woman to become aroused is *dyspareunia*, "painful or difficult intercourse," and gynecologists want their patients to have easy and pleasant intercourse so they'll get pregnant. But Ob-Gyns weren't going to concern themselves with questions of arousal unless its absence was a woman's presenting problem. Because women's pleasure is "excessive," not connected to fertility, in obstetrical-gynecological terms, it's doomed to remain a frill.

Women's sexuality is powerful and terrifying, not only our potential for reproduction but also our capacity for pleasure, the possibility of sequences or cascades of orgasms and the diffused sensations that enable various women to climax in multiple ways: from suckling, stroking, vaginal or anal intercourse, genital kisses, etc. An almost limitless potential for arousal resides within a woman's body, and she responds without the vulnerable insignia of a visible erect phallus.

Because women can hide our arousal response, if we wish, we can also mystify our sexuality. Many men suspect women of lying about bodily sexual events, which are subtler than the gross anatomy of erection and ejaculation. The truth about women's arousal and pleasure might be humiliating for men to face directly, so the official story involves erections and ejaculations, fertility and mirror responses: he gets an erection, they engage in foreplay, she

Arousal

becomes aroused, he stimulates her through intercourse, and they both climax. My fellow panelists weren't going to rock that boat.

Poets and writers, gay, lesbian, and straight, have written against this bias for a long time, but their celebrations of clitoral and anal pleasure have been relegated to the lavender ghetto where feminist, lesbian, and gay subject matter is presumed to appeal to special audiences. They certainly haven't affected the received truths of human sexuality as it's taught in medical schools.

During the very years I worked in that obstetrics and gynecology department, however, French feminist philosophers entered the zone of scientific silence and began to fill it with new speech based in women's bodies, the shapes of our genitalia. Language, these writers were proving, mirrors male reality. Cultural definitions of man, woman, and child have taken for granted that the index member of society is a man, and Woman is always a special case. We women may hold up half the sky, as the Chinese revolutionary slogan claims, but the mirror screen of language reflects back to us an artificial image, smaller than life.

Hélène Cixous, Julia Kristeva, and Luce Irigaray began the mighty intellectual labor of recentering human culture, opening language and flooding the imaginary, the image reservoir, with recognizable shapes and symbols for women's bodied experience. Their books, like *The Laugh of the Medusa* and *This Sex Which Is Not One,* have built a base for me to construct this one.

Possibilities

ONE SUMMER DAY IN THE 1980s, I walked down a country road under a blazing sun with a gaggle of small children, all of us wearing bathing suits and flip-flops. A shiny black car passed and repassed us, the driver lounging with his arm across the back of the front seat. I glanced at him; his eyes burned me, and I hustled the children off the road and down a dirt path to the quarry pond where we were going to swim. That dude looked dangerous. His license plate read SNAKE.

Snakes appear in Judeo-Christian culture as powerful, contradictory symbols, and I can't write about arousal and pleasure without considering them. Serpents are among the richest symbols in our cultural image reservoir;

Arousal

since before the beginning of writing, they have signified fertility, danger, good and bad luck, treachery, and prophecy, among other things.

Because there is evidence from Crete and elsewhere that worship of a great goddess involved snakes, some feminist historians say that stories about heroes conquering serpents could refer to the mythic moment when goddess worship yielded to the assaults of the male gods. Infant heroes like Heracles and Krishna fought snakes while still in their cradles, and St. Patrick drove snakes out of Ireland. If snakes were sacred animals in some prehistoric goddess religions, these myths could be seen as stories of the displacement of goddess worship in Greece, on the Subcontinent, and on the Emerald Isle.

In our culture, any sacred connection has decayed until the mere word *snake* on a license plate signals vulgar bragging and sexual danger. One of the few affirmative serpents that is recognized by at least some Westerners is Kundalini, the female serpent symbol of Tantric yoga. On a deep metaphorical level, sexual arousal is identified in Tantric practice with the awakening of Kundalini. The Kundalini energy symbolizes both the penis, which lengthens and swells like a roused serpent, and the vagina, which has muscles patterned in rings like a serpent's body and which opens into a hungering maw.

Monotheistic religions unified many gods into one, but they fragmented the notion of a human being. In Judaism, Christianity, and Islam, the human being is conceived as an assemblage of conflicting parts: a knowing head, a striving soul, an erring body, rather than an integral entity connected to earth and its other creatures. Most religious teachings assume that each human fragment has desires that conflict with the others: the body wants comfort and pleasure; the mind wants knowledge; the spirit wants goodness; and these aims are incompatible. What's more, at the time when these ideas took shape, it was assumed that the index human being was male. Women were always a special case: a special source of pleasure, a temptation, a "near occasion of sin," sometimes a repository of goodness, but very seldom a seeker after knowledge.

For monotheistic faiths, especially Christianity, with its explicit scorn for sexual pleasure, the power of arousal is evidence of the wayward body that must be controlled. Not a creative force that can fuel a satisfying life, but an irrepressible demon, the "old Adam" or "old Nick" that must be chastised and kept in the body's dungeon. Sky god worshipers mistrust the body, and they have invented a criminal code to control its most powerful impulses.

Other religions may not explicitly subordinate women, as Judaism, Christianity, and Islam have done, but in virtually all cultures the effect is similar. Buddhism and Hinduism hold out an ideal of transcendance in which bodily comfort and pleasure—associated with women as both mothers and lovers—lose meaning by comparison to spiritual enlightenment.

In some mystical practices, the human person can be a unified being, body-mind indivisible from spirit. Gnosticism

Arousal

and Kabbalah interpret sacred texts so that pagan wisdom can be reinscribed into monotheistic religious practice. In Kundalini yoga, the path to bliss and transcendance begins with cultivating the flow of creative energy that lives within every human being. Metaphorically, Kundalini lies coiled at the base of the spine and can be raised through each of the seven energy centers, or chakras, until her power fills the whole body.

Although the divine energy is conceptualized as a female serpent, in its classic form Kundalini yoga is a discipline for men. The classic texts, including the *Bhagavad-Gita,* mention women as subjects and objects of pleasure, but only men are subjects for enlightenment. Egalitarian modern Tantrics, of course, include women as practitioners.

Despite the efforts of modern popularizers to spread the Tantric wisdom, we as a culture (again, metaphorically) tread the Kundalini serpent underfoot and build for our sexual expression a domain of chastisement, shame, confinement, and agony that we call pleasure. The chakras describe a continuous path along which the creative energies can flow, but instead of nourishing the Kundalini energy and cherishing its gifts of arousal and pleasure, our culture cuts it into pieces. We divide ourselves in two, honoring head and heart and treating our lower quarters as though they belonged to another species. The "lower passions" live in the belly and pelvis, according to this scheme; their dirty organs are a source of shame, pain, disease. When the mad King Lear fulminated against women, he cried:

> *Down from*
> *The Waste they are Centaurs, though Women all above.*
> *But to the Girdle do the Gods inherit;*
> *Beneath is all the Fiends. There's Hell, there's Darkness,*
> *There is the Sulphurous Pit: burning, scalding*
> *Stench, Consumption . . .*

Then we behead ourselves as well, forfeiting our capacity to unite the body's creative energy with what we call our intellect and spirit. We fear wholeness. Language and philosophy encourage us to call our pleasures "sin" or "weakness." For fear of arousing our sleeping serpent, our sexual energy, we stifle our voices and choke off our breath; we paralyze our bowels and numb our genitals. We think of sexual expression as a toxic pleasure, like drugging; we conceptualize Kundalini as a viper.

Far from being "a sleep and a forgetting," human birth is a violent expulsion from abundance, from a state of systematic fulfillment, into the chill hardness of desire, of lack. Because human children have such long careers of helplessness, our consciousness and memory develop long before we have the mental or physical muscles for independent life, and our very earliest experiences print us with the texts of culture.

Having a child of one's own famously awakens all sorts of feelings that most adults put away, only to have them abruptly summoned by our sensory response to the baby. Infantile feelings have slept in the unconscious, folded

Arousal

into silence, opening occasionally in dreams but seldom surfacing. The velvet of close-grained baby skin, the sweet smell of baby sweat, the helpless greed of a sucking baby mouth reaches down inside us and touches that infant with its loose gender identity, its pleasures and rages.

A woman nursing her infant at her breast may find she responds to it like a lover; the suckling pressure of its gums and tongue lights up a neural pathway to her pelvis, to her vulva. Feminist scholar Lynda Marín writes, "What if one of the best-kept secrets is that there is no distinction, really, between motherly affection and female passion?"

Having the baby, caring for the baby, opens some of the old wounds we carry from our own infancy. A baby is a bundle of cravings, and no human infant ever got enough. We are all weaned from our mother's breasts, the marvelous feeding system Freud thought was "the most perfect" human relationship, and we all make different use of the rage we feel at this separation. But when you put a baby to your own breast, or when your lover puts a baby to the breast that gave you pleasure, forgotten feelings awaken, the thwarted cravings and the sadness and rage that go along with them.

Philip Slater, in *The Glory of Hera,* finds the shock of weaning, especially in cultures where children breastfeed for two or three years, reflected in tales of poison maidens and serpent-women. Analyst Melanie Klein based a whole theory of psychosexual development on what she called Good Breast/Bad Breast; the good breast is full of milk and available; the bad breast is empty or withheld. The ancient myth of Amazon warriors literalizes this figure, with its story of militant women who cut off one breast to make them better archers *(a* = not; *mazos* = breast) and suckled their female children with the remaining breast.

The closeness of these cravings and this rage helps to explain both woman-hating as a widespread characteristic of culture and the connection between pleasure and violence, which is so firm that hardly anyone even questions it. The roots of family violence, incest, child-beating, and woman-battering also plunge deep into the same territory: lovers and children touch what Griffin calls "the vulnerable feeling self," the hungering child that dwells inside each one of us, whose desires are still unslaked and whose shames and frustrations so often shape our adult expressions of those desires. For some of us, to feel desire and to become aroused awakens such degrading memories that only violence and pain can match our humiliated longing.

Arousal, the topic with which I began, describes an array of strong feelings connected to one another in such a way that when one wakes, others stir—lust and anger, jealousy and fear, joy and despair. What is aroused in us is simply our first feelings, the raw pains and pleasures of our infancy. When we respond physically to signs, smells, and caresses, it's because they touch our infant marrow. The pain that surrounds our pleasure—the rage or terror that inflects our sexual love—comes from the utter helplessness of that infant and that unprotected core. Childhood wounds and bruises surround it with painful scars. Blessedly, there are places in the body where the tender ancient self can be touched and pleasured, where the touch of smooth skin, warm lips, or clever fingers reaches a layer

Arousal

of feeling where we are infants once again, joyful, rageful, powerful center of the universe.

The problem with which I began, how to separate sexual pleasure from cruelty, especially cruelty to women, is another one of civilization's famous discontents. Children must be raised—brought up from the primitive state in which they're delivered—weaned and trained, clothed and taught, and even the most loving, careful upbringing will thwart a child's limitless desires. Children are eager to learn, to gain power in the world, but every new skill comes at the price of an old pleasure, like the pleasures of suckling, of letting go of body wastes, or of being warmly held and carried. A part of every child welcomes the new skills and the power they bring, but another part feels a residue of rage against the parents—most often the mothers—who must deny them the old satisfaction. We learn to read eagerly, but part of us resents not being read to.

The mother's power is experienced as domination, and one of the earliest games most children play is that they have power, too, that they can dominate others. Language is an early power tool: tiny tots order their parents around, they boss and brutalize their dolls and stuffed animals. Some children, if they're not stopped, go on to torment pets and bully one another.

These power-playing children also survive inside each of us, buried but untamed, caught in a web of anger and desire because the rule givers who thwarted us were also the source of our oldest pleasures. The first object of erotic feeling, the mother, is also the first object of helpless rage.

And most children learn new pleasures, conversions, and substitutes against the body and presence of a woman. The keen new pleasure of converting helpless rage to domination, for example, comes through the power of language and other social behavior.

Arousal begins at home, in our first home, in the intimacies of babyhood, and we store the memories our whole lives. Our earliest pleasures may come close to the perfection of life before birth, but we can never recapture it entirely. So pleasures teach us to want more, and when our wants are ignored or denied, we learn rage. The fact that children direct most of their desires and angers toward women accounts for why both men and women can take delight, at least in fantasy, in the binding and torment of female bodies.

In her important book, *The Mermaid and the Minotaur*, Dorothy Dinnerstein proposed that the basic reason why men should share child care is so that they may become equal objects of this rage and this desire. With the blinding speed of recent social change, this has in fact begun to happen. Changing patterns of work, education, and family life have changed gender assumptions, and the care and feeding of infants has become a shared project in many families. Even when women breastfeed their children, men share the schlepping, traffic control, toilet training, language learning, and other scut work of parenting.

If this continues, and more infants grow up associating both bliss and frustration with the bodies of both male and female parents, the balance of gender power will continue to shift. Most of our assumptions about gender are based

Arousal

on our upbringing, so that even as we consciously try to remake the way we raise our children, the children of each new generation are growing into adults with gender assumptions subtly different from ours. Rather than reproducing the way their parents raised them, children will continue the slow morphing of gender roles. Gradually, human beings may be remaking sexual pleasure, too, and basing it more on mutuality than domination.

In the course of these reflections, I've remembered a conversation that took place many years ago, when I was in college. It was the beginning of fall quarter, and I ran into a friend named Laurie whom I hadn't seen since the previous spring. He had something to tell me, he said excitedly. He had made love for the first time over the summer, and it had been wonderful. More than that, it had been an experience of the sublime. He said, "I don't see how anyone who's ever done that can ever do anything bad."

Our college fed us heavy doses of Plato and Aristotle, and we were constantly on the lookout for the Good. Now, over summer vacation, Laurie had found it. My own introduction to carnal love had been less ecstatic, but I was happy for him. Who was the girl? I asked. Were they in love? No, he said; she was older than he, and it had been a summer romance. Neither of them expected anything more, but they had had a glorious time together.

Does Laurie sound sickeningly naive? This little story still touches my heart. I've remembered his words all these years, his discovery of pleasure as a supreme goodness. I think I remember his so vividly because it was so different from my own.

For both general and specific reasons, the connection for me between cruelty and pleasure had been firmly welded into place by the time I began to have sex with other people, but I didn't manage either the cruelty or the pleasure very well. So many of us begin our erotic social lives confused about the kind of partners we desire! I chose gentle boys and men who turned out to be as confused and misinformed as I was, some of them gay or bisexual. We were desperately seeking the goodness that our young flesh hinted at, and we were all culturally resistant—or as we said then, maladjusted—to some degree, but we (or at least I) needed to look in a lot of the wrong places before we were ready to experience our bodies and their pleasures.

By the time I learned about pleasure, cruelty played a minor part in my fantasies, but it never disappeared. I discovered partners who were more appealing, people who made me laugh, who weren't afraid to play games, who looked at my body as I looked at theirs, tenderly and curiously, intent on exploring possibilities. I was lucky; I did finally understand that there isn't any right way to do sex, just people's bodies and the pleasures they can find.

This understanding contradicts all sorts of orthodoxies, from the gymnastics of the *Kama Sutra* (and yes, of Tantric yoga) to Deuteronomic prescriptions to Protestant decencies to Freud's peculiar notions. But after shedding quarts of tears and other body fluids in the course of grappling with sexual contradictions, I'm convinced it is the path to liberation. The Kundalini energy will rise if we welcome her.

What—aside from cruelty—are the magic triggers that

Arousal

arouse the desire for pleasure? What seasons pleasure with an extra fillip that allows it to culminate? In *Pornography and Silence,* Griffin describes a tradition of openness and generosity that doesn't punish or confine desire, a sensibility she glimpses in the poetry of Blake, Whitman, and Rilke and the early paintings of Franz Marc. I'd had some inkling of a different kind of erotic excitement, a generous warmth that opened me and made me feel receptive and all-embracing.

This warmth rose in me at summer camp, at morning flag-raising on a beautiful knoll when wind rippled the flag and chased little clouds through a smooth sky, and sunlight glistened on the lake below. I had a crush on one of the counselors, a boyish brown-haired girl whose eyes crinkled when she laughed. As we pledged allegiance to the flag / of the United States of America / and to the republic for which it stands, I added, "the right to sleep with cute boys" to "liberty and justice for all" and my heart swelled with patriotic gratitude for this freedom.

Now I wonder exactly what freedom I was extolling. I knew Charlie was a girl, but I was glad she looked like a boy, and I wanted to have a lover who looked like her. I loved my girlfriends, and their bodies fascinated me. We sunbathed in our underwear, shyly comparing ourselves, but I didn't long to touch and kiss them. I wanted pleasure from those weird creatures who were differently made. Curiosity pushed me toward boys, boys who looked like Charlie, and that brief shock of patriotism—or something.

That *something*—a vision of freedom—later led me to radical politics and to folk music, its sound track. The seeds of the sixties' social revolutions surely sprouted in the folk music revival of the fifties. We sang and strummed— love songs, work songs, songs of the Spanish Civil War— and coupled after hootenannies. Left politics, democratic socialism, held out a vision of thrilling beauty: We would achieve our revolution nonviolently, maybe electorally, and would abolish poverty and wealth, end racial prejudice, and answer the Woman Question.

A little later still, I discovered the political possibilities of theater and decided that theater, not politics, would be the best way to transform the world. Plays by Shaw and Brecht showed some of the changed relationships between men and women that revolution promised, and improvisations further freed me from stereotyped roles.

Some people, I knew, got the same warm, open feelings from religion that theater and politics gave me. I'd had sketchy religious education: a year or so at a Labor Zionist Sunday school, because a friend of my mother's was an enthusiast, and a couple of years in confirmation class at a Conservative temple with a good choir director. Later, friends who grew up in rural areas told me about the erotic pull of Christian revivals and camp meetings. It sounded good then and makes sense to me now—music, singing in crowds, shared beliefs, a sense of higher purpose. Good, strong stuff—I can feel it in the pit of my stomach as I write. If only those religions weren't built on the hatred of women.

Arousal

The blissful solidarities of music, politics, and theater showed the way to a different construction of sexuality, one built not on infantile pain and rage but on shared warmth and goodness. What I loved most about singing in a choir was hearing my alto section in close harmony against the treble and bass, following a different melodic path but never leaving entirely, sometimes supporting the treble like a drone and sometimes carrying the melody against a bass continuo. I wanted my erotic energy to flow like that, in its own fullness but responsive, joining harmoniously with others'. When a scene played well on stage, it had the same thrilling balance. If we could make love like that, I thought, we could change the world.

If we did succeed—women and men alike—in spreading our cruelty and longing equally between male and female bodies, what would our erotica look like? There is a sense in which pornography has played a liberatory role in the modern world, as Angela Carter says in *The Sadeian Woman*. Although pornography makes no attempt to uncouple rage from lust—in fact emphasizes the connection—it does break any tie of sexuality to reproduction, for both women and men. In monotheistic cultures, women's sexual expression is usually limited to our childbearing function. At the same time, in its name ("writings and drawings of whores") pornography constructs pleasure as a commodity and preserves an imbalance between the consumer and its paid provider, the whore—a woman or man whose body can be bought.

Liberated erotica would celebrate pleasure as mutuality. We now believe that sexual pleasure is heightened by the barriers we have set up—religious, social, and psychological. Desire is transgressive in its origins, we say; it's only right that society make laws to contain it. In Henry Miller's words, "A stiff prick has no conscience."

But what if the heightening of pleasure came not from the barrier but from our belief in it? What if desire, far from being "transgressive," chimed with our most deeply social selves, with the pleasure that bonds us to one another, that lets us sing and dance together? We might gently let go of our faith in transgression and find that the barriers culture has erected turn us off, not on. If we found a way to bring up children who love their bodies and pleasures, who welcome sexual arousal and energy, they might invent an erotics of consent along with forms of sexuality that go beyond our dreams.

Nothing has spoilt my belief in socialism, even through the rough changes of history, though these days I have a more modest estimate of the powers of art. Still, the vision of a just and equitable world can fill me with delight, even as it recedes. I believe these new forms could be part of my just and equitable world. At risk of sounding New Agey, I propose that releasing creative energy to transform our sexual selves might also release the power we need to make a social revolution. Immense destructive systems have blossomed out of our ingenuity, and although we understand that we have become hazardous to our own health, we don't seem to know how to change. Why couldn't this ingenuity and power lead us beyond the bleak romance of destruction?

Unbinding our sexual energy from the punishments we inflict on it has always seemed too risky. Because we've historically labeled sexuality as a disruptive force, every political upheaval has been accompanied by widespread fears of sexual license—not rape, which is a technique of war, but "unbridled" sexuality. In Judeo-Christian fantasy, the phrase *sexual license* usually masks a fear of female or gay male sexuality. License or permissiveness—erotic freedom—leads to the loosening or breaking of social ties, neglect of children, disrespect of parents, and flouting of laws.

In our age, spirituality and religion are coming to be seen as two separable aspects of the human spirit, religion having to do with common culture, observance, and customs, and spirituality having to do with "oceanic" feelings, the juice of ecstasy. We sometimes invest the forms of religion with the fluid of our spirit, but the connection isn't automatic. So the spiritual rebirth that will let us do what we need to do as a species isn't necessarily a religious one. What we must do is honor the spirit in the only form we know it—the body. Through bodies and pleasures we can glimpse the sacred.

Passions are the speech of our bodies, they are our vitality speaking. Desire for pleasure begins as desire for what keeps us alive: food, warmth, safety. Desire is boundless, and boundlessness frightens us. We long for the close fit of our first love's body, but our longing is crossed with anger and shame. We have lost the understanding that sexual pleasure might become a spiritual path on which we can express our best selves.

I would like to believe that in some cultures, at some epochs, humans reverenced our genitals as our connection to divinity's mysterious powers. I know that at present, because our culture teaches us to hate and fear the strong impulse to pleasure that is signaled by arousal, many of us are able to experience genital pleasure only in narratives of dominance and submission.

Those of us whose sexuality has formed in this way resist the notion of change. We have taught Kundalini the tricks of an escape artist; we nearly strangle her as the price of pleasure. We dam and distort the Kundalini energy, as though only by penning her up and using her to punish ourselves can we acknowledge her power in our lives. We spend vast energies on this deployment, energies that could nourish our gift for pleasure. If we were to give up the distortions that we inflict on the part of us that we allow to feel pleasure, would we be cast adrift? If we disarmed the sexual energy that we have dammed, diverted, and deployed like a military force, might it inundate us, flooding across the landscape of our bodies? How would we make it crest or fall? Would we be like actors without a script, like puppets without hands? Remaking the world means remaking eroticism so that we give up dominance and submission (however subtly we transform them), and we're afraid it won't feel good.

This is one reason why the feminist struggle for gender

Arousal

justice is such a long, difficult one. Remaking the world also means inventing a language for hidden desires, creating an imaginary of female pleasure, unblocking erotic energy so that it can stream without fear or anger through our vulnerable, pleasure-loving flesh. We need a new view of human possibility, a singing, dancing one that is based in acceptance rather than hatred of our bodies, in improvisation rather than scripts.

Can humans ever quench the blaze of rage while preserving our capacity for pleasure? Can we teach ourselves to love the body that is all we have of life, and to rediscover the world-changing power of the goodness that we glimpse in sexual pleasure? I believe we can.

If we took our capacity for pleasure seriously, we would understand that arousal is a generic response, like the raising of a peacock's beautiful fan. Opening ourselves to the possibility of pleasure opens us also to fear, anger, jealousy, and tears. Kundalini rises when we open ourselves; we're most powerful when most vulnerable. Purged of shame and violence, sexual expression could become for us all the source of goodness my friend Laurie found.

Each one of us is the expert on our own subject, and we are entitled to find and to use a specific language for our bodies and our pleasures. Then we must learn to respect one another's languages, believe in one another's reality. These two preliminary steps alone will take many years of time and light-years of energy, and perhaps they will help us to dismantle our deadly species games of consumption and destruction.

The remaking of sexuality can not only save the world, it can make a world worth saving.

Notes

Introducing Arousal

p. 7 Michel Foucault, *History of Sexuality: La Volonté de savoir,* vol. 1 (New York: Random House, 1978), 69.

p. 8 Ibid., 159.

p. 12 Stephen Jay Gould writes in "Genes on the Brain" *(An Urchin in the Storm,* New York: W. W. Norton, 1987, 112–13): "Every scientist, indeed every intelligent person, knows that human social behavior is a complex and individual mix of biological and social influences. The issue is not *whether* nature or nurture determines human behavior, for these factors are truly inextricable, but the degree, intensity, and nature of the constraint exerted by biology upon the possible forms of social organization."

pp. 16–17 Foucault, *History of Sexuality.*

Learning to Read

p. 21 Roland Barthes, "Fetish," in *The Pleasure of the Text,* trans. Richard Miller (New York: Hill & Wang, 1975), 27.

p. 22 Ibid., "Edges," 7.

p. 26 This argument appears in several of MacKinnon's works, including *Feminism Unmodified: Discourses on Life and Law* (Cambridge, Mass.: Harvard University Press, 1987), but I first heard her make it in a lecture at the University of Minnesota Law School in the fall of 1985. At the time MacKinnon was team-teaching a course on the legal status of pornography with writer Andrea Dworkin. It was in this class that they developed the model of pornography as a civil-rights violation, and the Minneapolis City Council adopted an antipornography statute drafted in their class, which was later vetoed by Mayor Don Fraser.

p. 26 Especially Carolee Schneemann, the pioneering feminist filmmaker and performance artist, in her film *Fuses* (1967) and her performance works, including *Meat Joy* (1964) and *Interior Scroll* (1975).

p. 26 For example, in Alexandra Kollontai's *Love of Worker Bees*—an early novel about Soviet revolutionaries—an idealistic heroine finds her hopes for equality of sexual opportunity and pleasure betrayed by her lovers.

p. 26 Lynne Segal, column in *Guardian International*, 7 Sept. 1994.

Sameness and Difference

p. 33 Critic Valerie Traub, in her book *Desire and Anxiety* (New York: Routledge & Kegan Paul, 1992, 100), which mainly deals with sexuality in Shakespeare's plays, puts the question thus: "When viewing a love scene on a movie screen . . . do you *want* or do you *want to be* one of the images on the screen? Which one? Can you tell?"

p. 34 Luce Irigaray, *This Sex Which Is Not One* (Ithaca, N.Y.: Cornell University Press, 1985), 220.

Notes

p. 35 This is said by the Alcharisi, an opera singer who is the mother of Daniel Deronda *(Daniel Deronda* in *George Eliot's Works,* vol. 10. Edinburgh: Blackwood, 1911, 345).

pp. 40–41 Leslie Feinberg, author of *Stone Butch Blues* (Ithaca, N.Y.: Firebrand Books, 1993) and *Transgender Warriors* (Boston: Beacon Press, 1996) spoke at Minneapolis's Amazon Bookstore in April, 1995.

p. 41 Wayne Koestenbaum, *The Queen's Throat: Opera, Homosexuality, and the Mystery of Desire* (New York: Vintage Books, 1993), 178.

p. 42 The article on Legos appeared in the *Globe & Mail,* 4 July 1995.

Desire

p. 47 Conversation with Judith Arcana, October, 1996, Portland, Oregon.

p. 58 Michael Flanders and Donald Swann were English singer-songwriters *(At the Drop of a Hat,* Angel Records, 1960). The refrain of their "Reluctant Cannibal" went as follows:
   Oh, you can't eat people
   Don't eat people
   Eating people is *wrong.*

p. 59 Charles Sherrington, *Integrative Action of the Nervous System* (New Haven: Yale University Press, 1920). See especially lecture 7, "Reflexes as Adapted Reactions," 262–3.

Silence

p. 64 The image of a headless classical goddess appears on the cover of the paperback edition of Janet Malcolm's

Arousal

biography of the poet Sylvia Plath, *The Silent Woman* (New York: Vintage, 1995). The title is ironic in the sense that Plath's death prevents her from entering the argument that still eddies, nudged from time to time by scholars or by her family members, around the facts of her life and death. In life she was not silent, although (and this is part of the argument) perhaps periodically silenced.

The image of a headless woman—apparently a woodcut of a peasant woman wearing an apron over her skirts—appeared for many years in the *New Yorker* magazine, in a small advertisement for a New England inn called The Silent Woman. The image disappeared from the ad sometime in the 1970s, though the inn continued to advertise in the magazine.

p. 68 Muriel Rukeyser, "Despisals," in *A Muriel Rukeyser Reader,* edited by Jan Heller Levi (New York: W. W. Norton, 1994). Copyright © 1994 by Jan Heller Levi and William Rukeyser. Also published in *Breaking Open* (New York: Random House, 1973). Reprinted with permission from William L. Rukeyser.

p. 68 Monique Wittig, *Les Guerrillères* (Paris: Editions de Minuit, 1969) and *Le Corps lesbien* (Paris: Editions de Minuit, 1973).

p. 68 This is certainly true of Courbet's "Girl with White Stockings" (Philadelphia: Barnes Collection), although there is a faint suggestion, in "L'Origine du Monde," of a pearly inner lip glimpsed within the dark cleft (Paris: Musée d'Orsay).

p. 68 Guy Hocquenghem, *Homosexual Desire* (London: Allison & Busby, 1978).

p. 69 Luce Irigaray, *This Sex Which Is Not One* (Ithaca, N.Y.: Cornell University Press, 1985).

p. 69 Luce Irigaray, "Blind Spot of an Old Dream of Symmetry," in *Speculum of the Other Woman* (Ithaca, N.Y.: Cornell University Press, 1985), 29.

Notes

p. 73 Ibid., 53.

p. 77 Lacan's reply was quoted to me by Peter Locke, who was in the audience. Jacques Lacan, who treated many artists including Pablo Picasso, once owned Courbet's "L'Origine du Monde." According to art historian Linda Nochlin, the painting hung in his country house, "La Prévoté," in Guitrancourt near Mantes-la-Jolie, as part of a diptych constructed by the artist Andre Masson. (Sarah Faunce and Linda Nochlin: *Courbet Reconsidered* [Brooklyn: The Brooklyn Museum, 1988], 178.)

p. 77 Irigaray, "Blind Spot of an Old Dream of Symmetry," in *Speculum of the Other Woman*.

p. 79 Ibid.

Cruelty

p. 83 Marcel Proust, *Within a Budding Grove* (New York: Random House, 1934), 359.

pp. 90–91 V. M. Hillyer and Edward G. Huey, *A Child's History of the World* (New York: Appleton-Century-Crofts, 1951), 94–95.

p. 93 Sylvia Plath, "Daddy," from *Ariel* (New York: Harper & Row, 1965), 49. Copyright © 1961, 1962, 1963, 1964, 1965 by Ted Hughes. Reprinted with permission from HarperCollins.

p. 97 See Denis Jackson, *The Price and Identification Guide to Alberto Varga and George Petty, Pin-up Artists* (Sequim, Wash.: TICN, 1992).

p. 99 Luce Irigaray, "Blind Spot of an Old Dream of Symmetry," in *Speculum of the Other Woman* (Ithaca, N.Y.: Cornell University Press, 1985), 125-26.

p. 99 Roland Barthes, "Tongue," in *The Pleasure of the Text* (New York: Hill & Wang, 1975), 37.

Arousal

p. 101 Linda Hogan, "Department of the Interior," in Patricia Foster, ed., *Minding the Body* (New York: Anchor Books, 1994), 167.

pp. 102–3 This joke, vividly remembered from my first reading of *Fefu* in about 1982, does not appear in any published edition. The play itself is in a sense an expansion of it (Maria Irene Fornés, *Fefu and Her Friends,* New York: PAJ Publications, 1990).

p. 104 John de St. Jorre, "The Unmasking of O," *New Yorker,* 1 Aug. 1994, 42–50.

p. 105 Susan Griffin, *Pornography and Silence* (New York: Harper & Row, 1981), 14. Griffin is not the first writer to make this observation, but hers is an eloquently argued part of a whole book on the erotic imagination, to which I am indebted for many insights.

Possibilities

p. 126 In medieval Christian art, serpents were a sign of the devil. Some images of the Virgin show her treading a snake under her feet. Serpents have come to signify dread, as in Emily Dickinson's "zero at the bone." In Western cultures, snakes have no positive connotations, but in Asian cultures, where ambiguity may be better tolerated than Western monotheisms, serpents and especially dragons symbolize power, creativity, change, and good fortune.

p. 126 In at least one feminist interpretation, the fire-breathing, maiden-menacing dragon of folklore represents female desire, while the armored knight who "rescues" the menaced maiden personifies the deployment of phallic sexuality—here seen as an opponent of the desiring woman.

p. 128 Sexual expression can be a form of meditation in Kundalini yoga. Partners who have prepared themselves to consecrate their shared love and pleasure, caring for their bodies by disciplined breathing, exercise, and diet, and learning to meditate on the forms, sounds, and colors belonging to each chakra, together can raise the sacred serpent the length of the spinal column. In this way, the sexual expression of their love is indissolubly physical and spiritual, and their erotic energy flows in an undammed stream.

p. 129 William Shakespeare, *King Lear,* act 4, sc. vi, lines 122–26.

p. 130 Lynda Marín, "Mother and Child: The Erotic Bond," in *Mother Journeys: Feminists Write about Mothering,* ed. Maureen T. Reddy, Martha Roth, and Amy R. Sheldon (Duluth, Minn.: Spinsters Ink, 1994), 13.

p. 131 Since Amazons reared only their female children and sent male infants away or sold them into slavery, even the single remaining breast of an Amazon represents, for men, a "bad" breast. The "good" breast, in this formulation, is the missing one—another instance of female lack.

p. 131 Susan Griffin, *Pornography and Silence* (New York: Harper & Row, 1981).

p. 136 Ibid.

p. 139 Henry Miller, *Tropic of Cancer* (New York: Grove Press, 1961).

p. 140 Susan Brownmiller proved this in her landmark 1975 study *Against Our Will: Men, Women, and Rape* (New York: Simon & Schuster, 1975). Her work has stimulated a worldwide response to war crimes against women.

p. 140 See, for example, the absurd, homophobic biblical story of Sodom and Gomorrah, Gen. 19. And remember the storm Dr. Joycelyn Elders kicked up when she was surgeon general with the mere hint that it might be good to include information about masturbation in sex education classes for young children.

Suggested Reading

Aeschylus. *Oresteia*. Translated by David Grene and Wendy Doniger O'Flaherty. Chicago: University of Chicago Press, 1989.

Anand, Margo. *The Art of Sexual Ecstasy*. San Francisco: HarperSanFrancisco, 1990.

Arcana, Judith. *Every Mother's Son*. New York: Anchor Press/Doubleday, 1983.

Barthes, Roland. *The Pleasure of the Text*. Translated by Richard Miller. New York: Hill & Wang, 1975.

Bersani, Leo. "Is the Rectum a Grave?" *October* 43 (Winter 1987).

Birken, Lawrence. *Consuming Desire: Sexual Science and the Emergence of a Culture of Abundance, 1871-1914*. Ithaca, N.Y.: Cornell University Press, 1988.

Brownmiller, Susan. *Against Our Will: Men, Women, and Rape*. New York: Simon & Schuster, 1975.

Arousal

Buchwald, Emilie, Pamela R. Fletcher, and Martha Roth, eds. *Transforming a Rape Culture*. Minneapolis: Milkweed Editions, 1993.

Burroughs, William. *Naked Lunch*. New York: Grove, 1984.

Butler, Judith. *Gender Trouble*. New York: Routledge, 1990.

———. *Bodies That Matter: On the Discursive Limits of 'Sex'*. New York: Routledge, 1993.

Bynum, Caroline Walker. *Holy Feast and Holy Fast: The Religious Significance of Food to Medieval Women*. Berkeley: University of California Press, 1987.

Carter, Angela. *The Sadeian Woman and the Ideology of Pornography*. New York: Pantheon, 1978.

Case, Sue-Ellen. "Towards a Butch-Femme Aesthetic." *Discourse* 11, no. 1 (1988–89).

Cixous, Hélène. *The Hélène Cixous Reader*. Edited by Susan Sellers. New York: Routledge, 1994.

———, and Catherine Clément. *The Newly Born Woman*. Translated by Betsy Wing. Minneapolis: University of Minnesota Press, 1986.

Clément, Catherine. *Opera, or the Undoing of Women*. Minneapolis: University of Minnesota Press, 1988.

Covington, Dennis. *Salvation on Snake Mountain: Snake Handling and Redemption in Southern Appalachia*. New York: Penguin, 1996.

Darwin, Charles. *The Expression of the Emotions in Man and Animals*. Chicago: University of Chicago Press, 1965.

D'Emilio, John, and Estelle Freedman. *Intimate Matters: A History of Sexuality in America*. New York: Harper & Row, 1988.

Derrida, Jacques. *Of Grammatology*. Translated by G. C. Spivak. Baltimore: Johns Hopkins University Press, 1976.

———. *Writing and Difference*. Translated by Alan Bass. Chicago: University of Chicago Press, 1978.

Suggested Reading

Dinnerstein, Dorothy. *The Mermaid and the Minotaur: Sexual Arrangements and Human Malaise.* New York: Harper Perennial, 1991.

Duberman, Martin Bauml, Martha Vicinus, and George Chauncey, Jr., eds. *Hidden from History: Reclaiming the Gay and Lesbian Past.* New York: NAL Books, 1989.

Dworkin, Andrea. *Woman Hating.* New York: Dutton, 1974.

Eisler, Riane. *Sacred Pleasure: Sex, Myth, and the Politics of the Body—New Paths to Power and Love.* San Francisco: HarperSanFrancisco, 1995.

Eliot, George. *Daniel Deronda.* Oxford: Oxford University Press, 1984.

Engels, Frederick. *The Origin of the Family, Private Property, and the State.* Edited by Eleanor Leacock. New York: Pathfinder Press, 1972.

Ferris, Lesley, ed. *Crossing the Stage: Controversies on Cross-Dressing.* New York: Routledge, 1993.

Foster, Patricia, ed. *Minding the Body: Women Writers on Body and Soul.* New York: Anchor Books, 1994.

Foucault, Michel. *History of Sexuality.* Vol. 1, *An Introduction.* New York: Random House, 1978.

———. Vol. 3: *The Care of the Self.* New York: Vintage, 1986.

———. *Birth of the Clinic: An Archaeology of Medical Perception.* Translated by A. M. Sheridan Smith. New York: Vintage Books, 1994.

Freud, Sigmund. *Collected Papers.* Vols. 1–4. London: Hogarth Press and the Institute of Psycho-Analysis, 1948.

Fuss, Diana. *Essentially Speaking: Feminism, Nature and Difference.* New York: Routledge, 1989.

Garber, Marjorie. *Vested Interests: Cross-Dressing and Cultural Anxiety.* New York: Routledge, 1992.

Arousal

Gay, Peter. *Freud: A Life for Our Time.* New York: W. W. Norton & Co., 1988.

Gilman, Charlotte Perkins. *The Yellow Wallpaper.* New Brunswick, N.J.: Rutgers University Press, 1993.

Gimbutas, Marija. *The Language of the Goddess.* New York: Harper & Row, 1989.

Gould, Stephen Jay. *An Urchin in the Storm: Essays about Books and Ideas.* New York: Norton, 1987.

———. *The Mismeasure of Man.* New York: W. W. Norton, 1996.

———. *Wonderful Life.* New York: W. W. Norton, 1989.

Graves, Robert. *Greek Myths.* 4th ed. London: Cassell, 1969.

———, and Raphael Patai. *Hebrew Myths: The Book of Genesis.* New York: Doubleday, 1963.

Griffin, Susan. *Pornography and Silence: Culture's Revenge Against Nature.* New York: Harper & Row, 1981.

———. *Woman and Nature: The Roaring Inside Her.* New York: Harper & Row, 1978.

Howard, Jean. "Cross-dressing, the Theatre, and Gender Struggle in Early Modern England." *Shakespeare Quarterly* 39, no. 4 (1988).

Homer. *The Iliad.* Translated by Robert Fitzgerald. New York: Doubleday, 1974.

Irigaray, Luce. "Blind Spot of an Old Dream of Symmetry." In *Speculum of the Other Woman.* Translated by Gillian C. Gill. Ithaca, N.Y.: Cornell University Press, 1985.

———. *This Sex Which Is Not One.* Translated by Catherine Porter. Ithaca, N.Y.: Cornell University Press, 1985.

Irvine, Janice. *Disordering Desire: Sex and Gender in Modern American Sexology.* Philadelphia: Temple University Press, 1990.

Jackson, Denis. *The Price and Indentification Guide to Alberto Varga and George Petty, Pin-up Artists.* Sequim, Wash.: TICN, 1992.

Suggested Reading

Jong, Erica. *Fear of Flying.* New York: Holt, Rinehart & Winston, 1973.

Keuls, Eva. *The Reign of the Phallus.* Berkeley: University of California Press, 1985.

Koestenbaum, Wayne. *The Queen's Throat: Opera, Homosexuality, and the Mystery of Desire.* New York: Poseidon Press, 1993.

Kollontai, Alexandra. *Love of Worker Bees.* Translated by Cathy Porter. New York: Academy Press, 1978.

Kristeva, Julia. *The Kristeva Reader.* Edited by Toril Moi. New York: Columbia University Press, 1986.

Lacan, Jacques. *Ecrits: A Selection.* New York: W. W. Norton, 1977.

Laqueur, Thomas. *Making Sex: Body and Gender from the Greeks to Freud.* Cambridge: Harvard University Press, 1990.

Leonardi, Susan J., and Rebecca A. Pope. *The Diva's Mouth: Body, Voice, Prima Donna Politics.* New Brunswick, N.J.: Rutgers University Press, 1996.

Licata, Salvatore J., and Robert P. Peterson. *The Gay Past: A Collection of Historical Essays.* New York: Harrington Park Press, 1986.

Lillehoj, Elizabeth. "Woman as Viewed by Man in Japanese Art." Exhibition catalog. Chicago: DePaul University, Field Museum, and Smart Museum of Art, 1995.

Lorde, Audre. *Uses of the Erotic: The Erotic as Power.* Brooklyn, N.Y.: Out & Out Books, 1978.

Lorenz, Konrad. *The Motivation of Human and Animal Behavior: An Ethological View.* New York: Van Nostrand & Reinhold Co., 1973.

———. *Behind the Mirror: A Search for a Natural History of Human Knowledge.* Translated by Ronald Taylor. London: Methuen, 1977.

MacKinnon, Catharine A. *Feminism Unmodified: Discourses on Life and Law.* Cambridge: Harvard University Press, 1987.

Arousal

Masters, William H., and Virginia E. Johnson. *Human Sexual Response*. Boston: Little, Brown, 1966.

Masters, William H., and Virginia E. Johnson, with Robert J. Levin. *The Pleasure Bond: A New Look at Sexuality and Commitment*. Boston: Little, Brown, 1974.

McClary, Susan. *Feminine Endings: Music, Gender, and Sexuality*. Minneapolis: University of Minnesota Press, 1991.

Milam, Lorenzo. *CripZen: A Manual for Survival*. San Diego: MHO & MHO Works, 1993.

Miller, James. *The Passion of Michel Foucault*. New York: Simon & Schuster, 1993.

Mitchell, Juliet. *Psychoanalysis and Feminism*. New York: Pantheon, 1974.

Mulvey, Laura. *Visual and Other Pleasures*. Bloomington: Indiana University Press, 1989.

Neumann, Erich. *The Great Mother: An Analysis of the Archetype*. Translated by Ralph Mannheim. Bollingen Series, vol. 47. Princeton, N.J.: Princeton University Press, 1964.

Oldfield, M. Howey. *The Encircled Serpent: A Study of Serpent Symbolism in All Countries and Ages*. London: Rider & Co., 1926.

Orgel, Stephen. "Nobody's Perfect: Or Why Did the English Stage Take Boys for Women?" *South Atlantic Quarterly* 88, no. 1 (1989).

Proust, Marcel. *Swann's Way*. Translated by C. K. Scott Moncrieff. New York: Random House, 1934.

———. *Within a Budding Grove*. Translated by C. K. Scott Moncrieff. New York: Random House, 1934.

Radway, Janice. *Reading the Romance: Women, Patriarchy, and Popular Literature*. Chapel Hill: University of North Carolina Press, 1984.

Reddy, Maureen T., Martha Roth, and Amy R. Sheldon, eds. *Mother Journeys: Feminists Write about Mothering*. Duluth: Spinsters Ink, 1994.

Suggested Reading

Rubin, Gayle. "The Traffic in Women: Notes on the 'Political Economy' of Sex." In *Feminist Frameworks*. Edited by Alison M. Jaggar and Paula S. Rothenberg. New York: McGraw-Hill, 1984.

Rukeyser, Muriel. *Breaking Open*. New York: Random House, 1973.

Scarry, Elaine. *The Body in Pain: The Making and Unmaking of the World*. Oxford: Oxford University Press, 1985.

———. *Resisting Representation*. Oxford: Oxford University Press, 1994.

Schneemann, Carolee. *More Than Meat Joy: Complete Performance Works and Selected Writings*. Edited by Bruce McPherson. New Paltz, N.Y.: Documentext, 1979.

Segal, Hanna. *Introduction to the Work of Melanie Klein*. New York: Basic Books, 1964.

Segal, Lynne. *Straight Sex: The Politics of Pleasure*. London: Virago, 1994.

The Sexual Subject: A Screen Reader in Sexuality. New York: Routledge, 1992.

Sherfey, Mary Jane. *The Nature and Evolution of Female Sexuality*. New York: Vintage, 1973.

Shulman, Alix Kates. *Memoirs of an Ex-Prom Queen*. New York: Alfred A. Knopf, 1972.

Sjöö, Monica, and Barbara Mor. *The Great Cosmic Mother: Rediscovering the Religion of the Earth*. San Francisco: HarperSanFrancisco, 1991.

Slater, Philip E. *The Glory of Hera: Greek Mythology and the Greek Family*. Boston: Beacon, 1968.

Smith, Joan. "People Eaters." *GRANTA* 52 (Winter 1995).

Snitow, Ann, Christine Stansell, and Sharon Thompson, eds. *Powers of Desire: The Politics of Sexuality*. New York: Monthly Review Press, 1983.

Spivak, Gayatri Chakravorty. *In Other Worlds: Essays in Cultural Politics.* New York: Routledge, 1988.

Sprengnether, Madelon. *The Spectral Mother: Freud, Feminism, and Psychoanalysis.* Ithaca, N.Y.: Cornell University Press, 1990.

Sprinkle, Annie, with Katherine Gates. *Annie Sprinkle's Post-Modern Pin-Ups Booklet.* San Francisco: Gates of Heck, 1995.

Stoller, Robert. *Observing the Erotic Imagination.* New Haven, N.J.: Yale University Press, 1985.

Stoltenberg, John. *Refusing to Be a Man: Essays on Sex and Justice.* New York: Penguin/Meridian, 1990.

Thomas, Lewis. *The Lives of a Cell: Notes of a Biology Watcher.* New York: Viking, 1974.

Thompson, William Irwin. *The Time Falling Bodies Take To Light: Mythology, Sexuality, and the Origin of Culture.* New York: St. Martin's Press, 1981.

Traub, Valerie. *Desire and Anxiety: Circulations of Sexuality in Shakespearean Drama.* New York: Routledge, 1992.

Vance, Carole S., ed. *Pleasure and Danger: Exploring Female Sexuality.* New York: Routledge & Kegan Paul, 1984.

Varga, Alberto. *Varga: The Esquire Years.* New York: Alfred Van Der Mark Editions, 1987 (1940).

Vishnudevananda, Swami. *The Complete Illustrated Book of Yoga.* The Julian Press, 1960.

Visser, Margaret. "The Sins of the Flesh." *GRANTA* 52 (Winter 1995).

Walker, Barbara G. *The Woman's Dictionary of Symbols and Sacred Objects.* San Francisco: Harper & Row, 1988.

Weeks, Jeffrey. *Sex, Politics, and Society: The Regulation of Sexuality Since 1800.* New York: Longman, 1981.

———. *Sexuality and Its Discourses.* London: Routledge & Kegan Paul, 1985.

Suggested Reading

Wittig, Monique. *Les Guerrillères*. Paris: Editions de Minuit, 1969.

———. *Le Corps lesbien*. Paris: Editions de Minuit, 1973.

Woolf, Virginia. *A Room of One's Own*. New York: Harcourt, Brace & World, 1957.

Yalom, Marilyn. *A History of the Breast*. New York: Knopf, 1997.

Born in Chicago and educated in public schools, the University of Chicago, and the université de Paris (Sorbonne), MARTHA ROTH worked for many years as a medical and scientific editor. She helped to found *Hurricane Alice: A Feminist Quarterly,* and most of her work concerns relations of power and pleasure between women and men. She has coedited two collections, *Transforming a Rape Culture* (Milkweed Editions, 1993) and *Mother Journeys: Feminists Write about Mothering* (Spinsters Ink, 1994). Her novel *Goodness* was published in 1996 by Spinsters Ink. She is married to Marty Roth, and they have two daughters and one son.

Interior design by Will Powers
Typeset in Sabon
by Stanton Publication Services, Inc.
Printed on acid-free 55# Sebago Antique Cream paper
by Maple-Vail Book Manufacturing

More nonfiction from Milkweed Editions

Changing the Bully Who Rules the World:
Reading and Thinking about Ethics
Carol Bly

The Passionate, Accurate Story:
Making Your Heart's Truth into Literature
Carol Bly

Transforming a Rape Culture
Edited by Emilie Buchwald, Pamela Fletcher, and Martha Roth

Rooms in the House of Stone
Michael Dorris

The Most Wonderful Books:
Writers on Discovering the Pleasures of Reading
Edited by Michael Dorris and Emilie Buchwald

Boundary Waters:
The Grace of the Wild
Paul Gruchow

Grass Roots:
The Universe of Home
Paul Gruchow

The Mythic Family
Judith Guest

The Art of Writing:
Lu Chi's Wen Fu
Translated from the Chinese by Sam Hamill

Chasing Hellhounds:
A Teacher Learns from His Students
Marvin Hoffman

Coming Home Crazy:
An Alphabet of China Essays
Bill Holm

The Heart Can Be Filled Anywhere on Earth:
Minneota, Minnesota
Bill Holm

Shedding Life:
Disease, Politics, and Other Human Conditions
Miroslav Holub

Rescuing Little Roundhead
Syl Jones

I Won't Learn from You!
The Role of Assent in Learning
Herbert Kohl

Basic Needs:
A Year with Street Kids in a City School
Julie Landsman

Tips for Creating a Manageable Classroom:
Understanding Your Students' Basic Needs
Julie Landsman

The Old Bridge:
The Third Balkan War and the Age of the Refugee
Christopher Merrill

Planning to Stay:
Learning to See the Physical Features of Your Neighborhood
William R. Morrish and Catherine R. Brown

Homestead
Annick Smith

What Makes Pornography "Sexy"?
John Stoltenberg

Testimony:
Writers of the West Speak On Behalf of Utah Wilderness
Compiled by Steve Trimble and Terry Tempest Williams